I am so *peaceful*

Sky Hawk

Published by Uiri Press 2016
First edition, first printing

Design and writing © 2016 Sky Hawk

All rights reserved. No part of this book may be reproduced or transmitted in any form or by any means, including but not limited to information storage and retrieval systems, electronic, mechanical, photocopy, recording, etc. without written permission from the copyright holder.

ISBN; 978-0-9979051-2-0

Dedication

To deep breaths, long exhales, warm cups
of tea and hot baths.

How To Use This Book

This is a 42 day journal that is focused on cultivating more peace in your life!

1. Read the quote and take some time to contemplate upon it. I like to use these for a daily focus.

2. Write down all the thoughts that are running around inside your head. These thoughts can be very distracting and it is often the same ones going on and on. Release them! Make an intention to let them go as you write.

3. Give yourself time for activities that brings you peace. This can be meditating, washing dishes while being in the present moment, taking a walk outside, etc.

4. The elliptical shape is where you will engage in art therapy. Take up some crayons, markers, or colored pencils and draw your feelings. This can look like a picture or scribbles. It is not about looking good. It is the expression of what is inside you. Try not to judge it. Just let it go and have fun.

5. Every seventh day there will be a weekly review. On the right hand page you will write a letter to someone you need to forgive. This may be another being or yourself. Then fill in the gratitude meter by shading in where you feel you are at. "I feel like I am going to scream", is 0, "I am like a cloud floating on a breeze", is 10. Remember your daily actions and reflect on your peaceful life.

> *Watch your manner of speech if you wish to develop a peaceful state of mind. Start each day by affirming peaceful, contented and happy attitudes and your days will tend to be pleasant and successful.*
> *Norman Vincent Peale*

Write down all those thoughts that are weighing you down. Then let them go.

(optional; cross them out with black ink or do whatever you need to do to let them go)

Make time for peaceful activities.
An action that brought me peace today was...

_____
_____
_____
_____
_____
_____
_____
_____
_____
_____

Art Therapy
Give yourself some time to scribble out those feelings. Either purposefully draw a picture or grab a color, close your eyes and let your mind go.

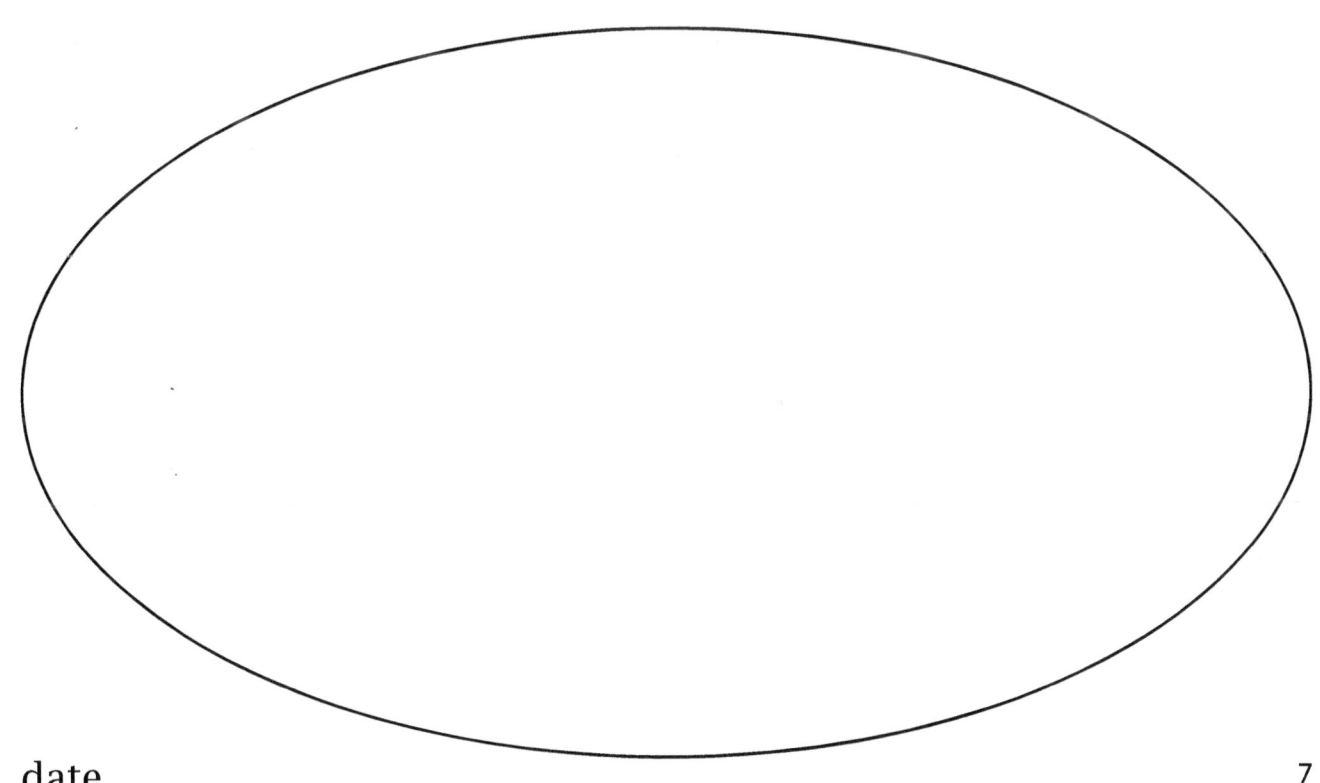

date_____

> *Just as treasures are uncovered from the earth, so virtue appears from good deeds, and wisdom appears from a pure and peaceful mind. To walk safely through the maze of human life, one needs the light of wisdom and the guidance of virtue.*
> *Buddha*

Write down all those thoughts that are weighing you down. Then let them go.
(optional; cross them out with black ink or do whatever you need to do to let them go)

_____
_____
_____
_____
_____
_____
_____
_____
_____
_____
_____
_____
_____
_____
_____
_____
_____

Make time for peaceful activities.
An action that brought me peace today was...

_____
_____
_____
_____
_____
_____
_____
_____
_____
_____

Art Therapy
Give yourself some time to scribble out those feelings. Either purposefully draw a picture or grab a color, close your eyes and let your mind go.

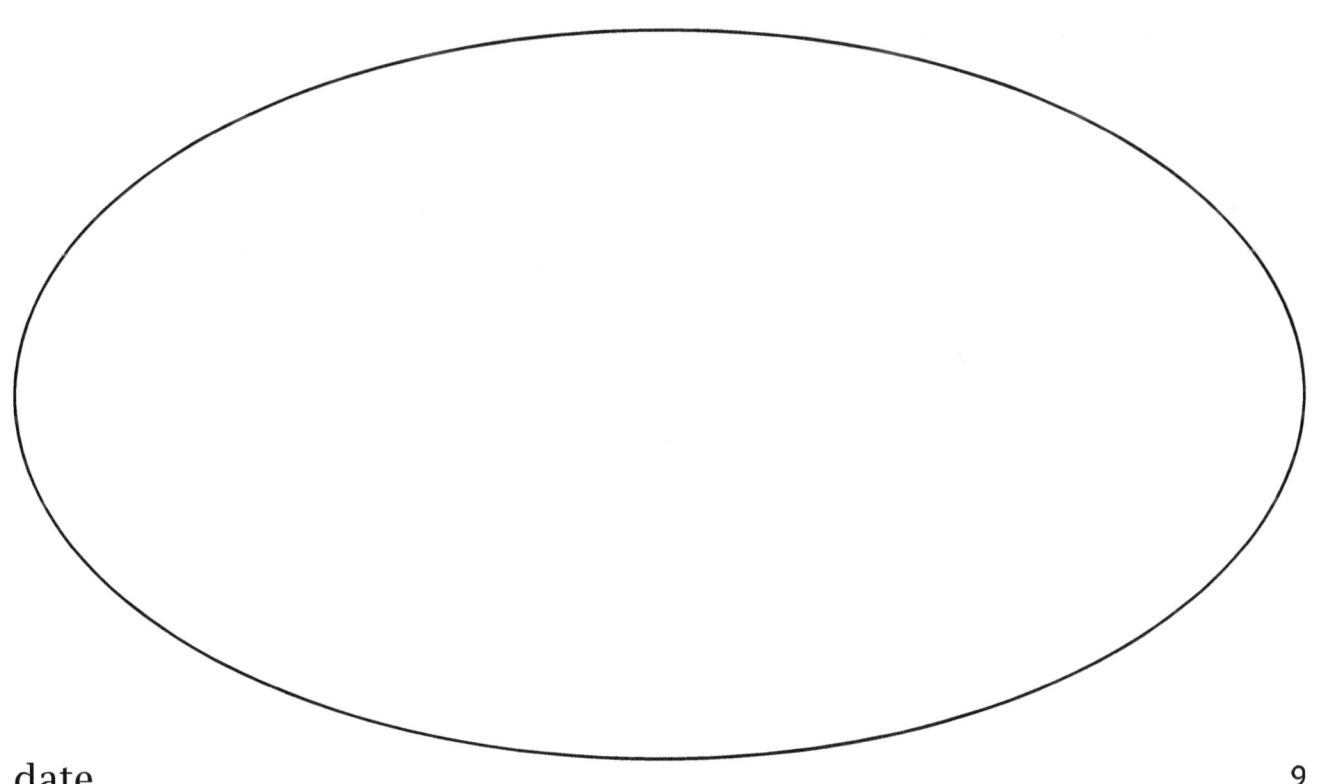

date_____

> *Letting go helps us to live in a more peaceful state of mind and helps restore our balance. It allows others to be responsible for themselves and for us to take our hands off situations that do not belong to us. This frees us from unnecessary stress.*
> *Melody Beattie*

Write down all those thoughts that are weighing you down. Then let them go.
(optional; cross them out with black ink or do whatever you need to do to let them go)

_____
_____
_____
_____
_____
_____
_____
_____
_____
_____
_____
_____
_____
_____
_____
_____
_____
_____
_____

Make time for peaceful activities.
An action that brought me peace today was...

_____
_____
_____
_____
_____
_____
_____
_____
_____
_____

Art Therapy
Give yourself some time to scribble out those feelings. Either purposefully draw a picture or grab a color, close your eyes and let your mind go.

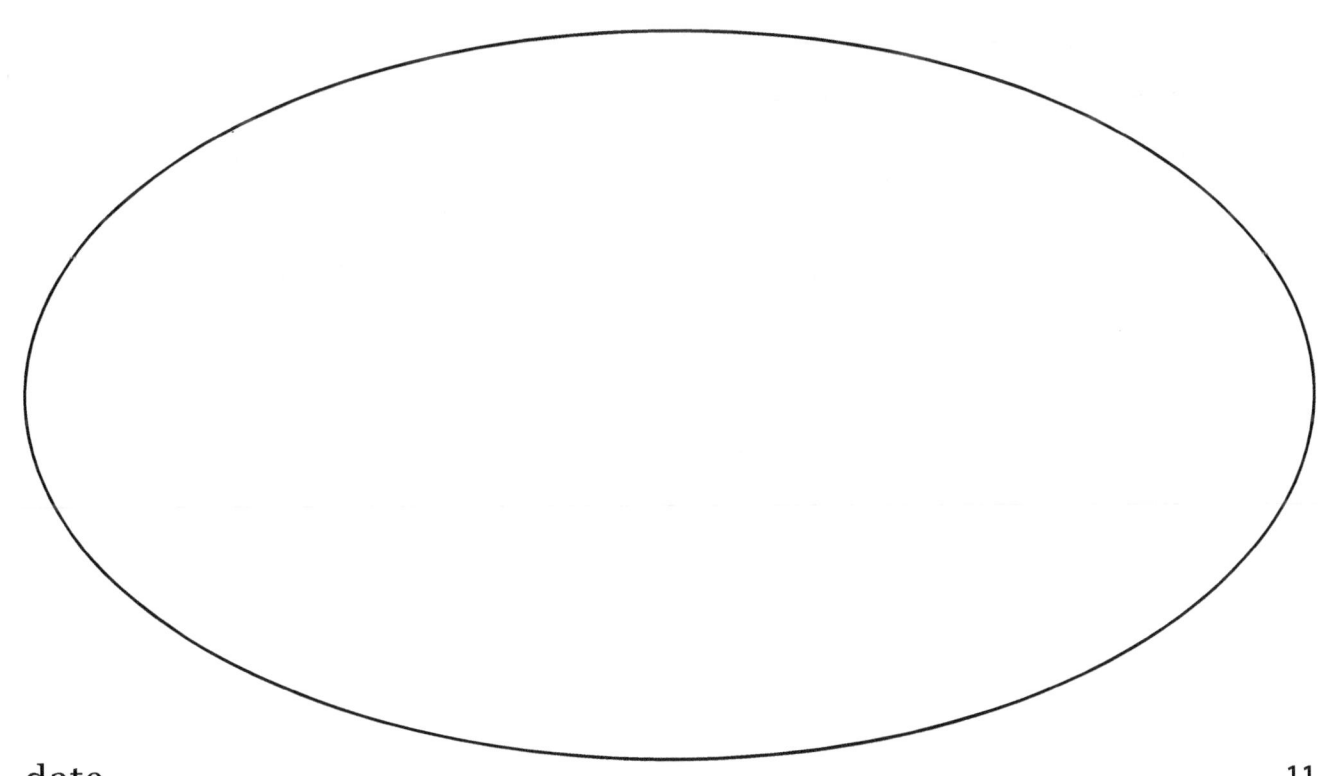

date_____

> *Mother Nature is always speaking. She speaks in a language understood within the peaceful mind of the sincere observer. Leopards, cobras, monkeys, rivers and trees; they all served as my teachers when I lived as a wanderer in the Himalayan foothills.*
> *Radhanath Swami*

Write down all those thoughts that are weighing you down. Then let them go.
(optional; cross them out with black ink or do whatever you need to do to let them go)

Make time for peaceful activities.
An action that brought me peace today was...

_____
_____
_____
_____
_____
_____
_____
_____
_____
_____

Art Therapy
Give yourself some time to scribble out those feelings. Either purposefully draw a picture or grab a color, close your eyes and let your mind go.

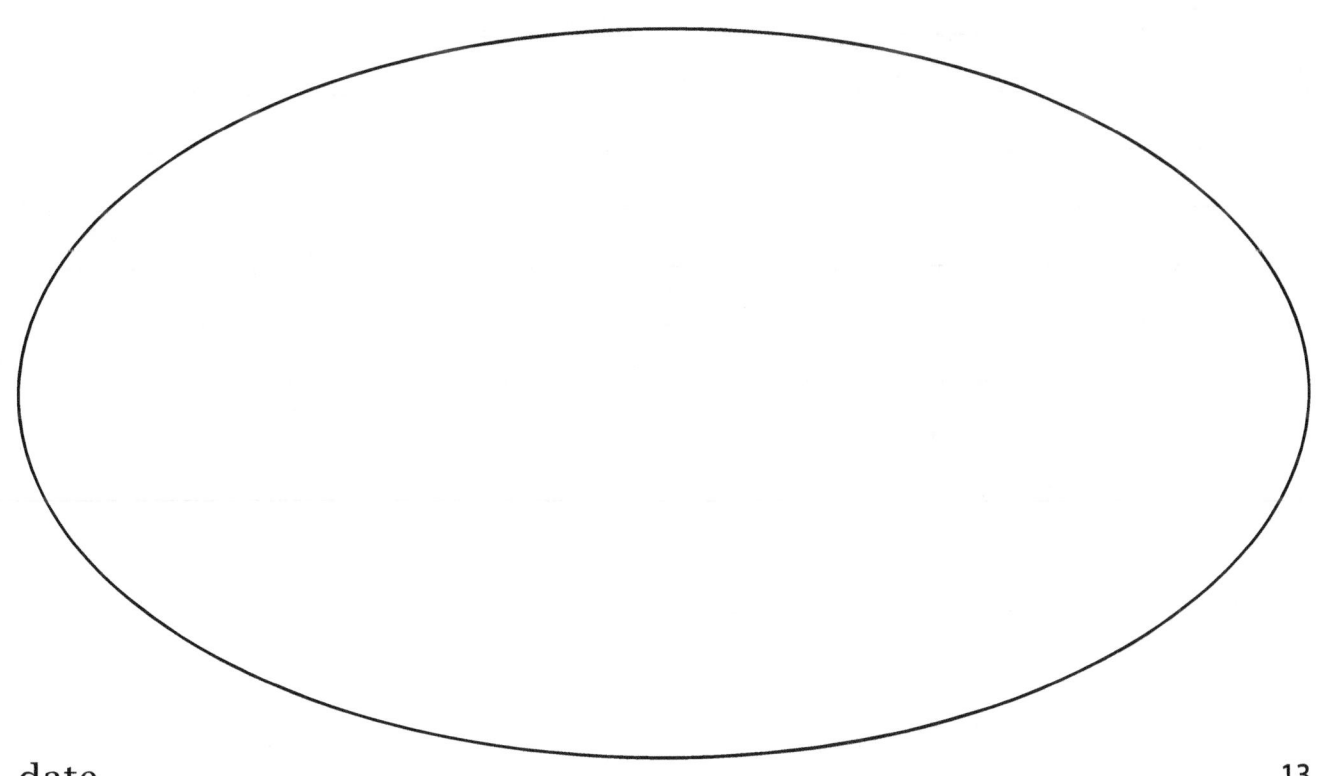

date_____

> *Appearance is something absolute, but reality is not that way - everything is interdependent, not absolute. So that view is very helpful to maintain a peace of mind because the main destroyer of a peaceful mind is anger.*
> *Dalai Lama*

Write down all those thoughts that are weighing you down. Then let them go.
(optional; cross them out with black ink or do whatever you need to do to let them go)

_____
_____
_____
_____
_____
_____
_____
_____
_____
_____
_____
_____
_____
_____
_____
_____
_____
_____

Make time for peaceful activities.
An action that brought me peace today was...

_____
_____
_____
_____
_____
_____
_____
_____
_____
_____

Art Therapy
Give yourself some time to scribble out those feelings. Either purposefully draw a picture or grab a color, close your eyes and let your mind go.

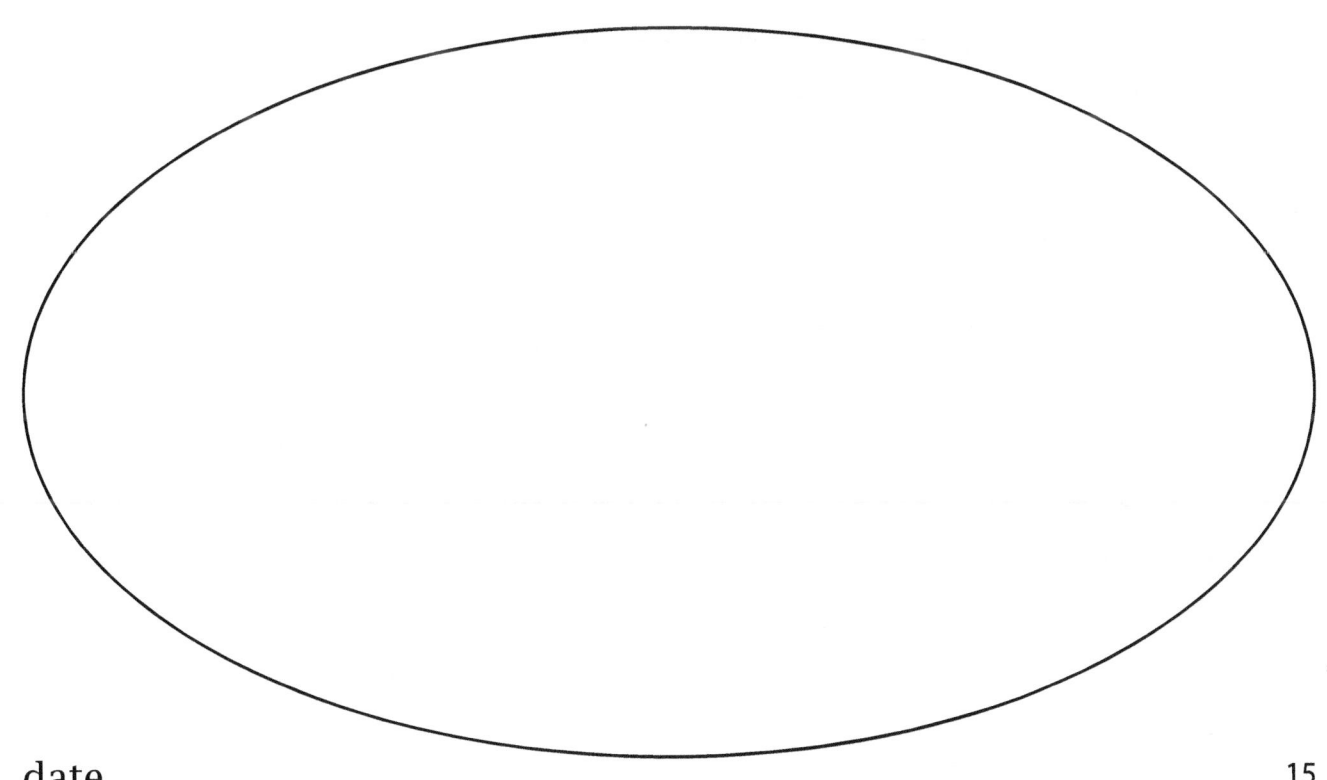

date_____

> *Lord, make me an instrument of thy peace.*
> *Where there is hatred, let me sow love.*
> *Francis of Assisi*

Write down all those thoughts that are weighing you down. Then let them go.
(optional; cross them out with black ink or do whatever you need to do to let them go)

Make time for peaceful activities.
An action that brought me peace today was...

_____
_____
_____
_____
_____
_____
_____
_____
_____
_____

Art Therapy
Give yourself some time to scribble out those feelings. Either purposefully draw a picture or grab a color, close your eyes and let your mind go.

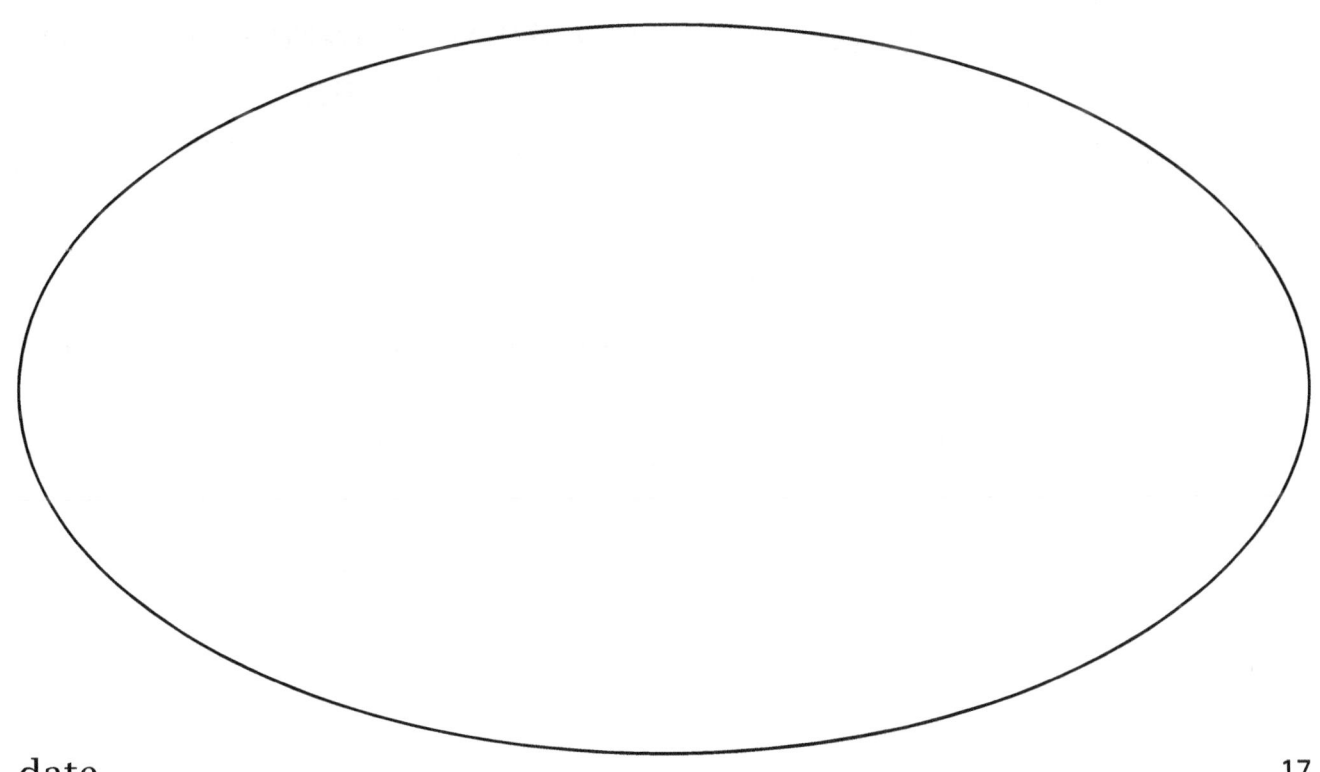

date_____

What a week! I love my peaceful journal.

Write down the difference you notice in your life as you have been focused on peace.

_____
_____
_____
_____
_____
_____
_____
_____
_____
_____
_____
_____
_____
_____
_____
_____
_____
_____

*Peace is a journey of a thousand miles
and it must be taken one step at a time.
Lyndon B. Johnson*

**** *My daily peaceful actions* ****

_____
_____
_____
_____

Dear _____

I have something I need to tell you. I forgive you for...

_____
_____
_____
_____
_____
_____
_____
_____
_____
_____
_____
_____
_____
_____
_____
_____
_____
_____
_____

peaceful meter

| I think I am going to scream | | I am like a cloud floating on a breeze |

> *To enjoy good health, to bring true happiness to one's family, to bring peace to all, one must first discipline and control one's own mind. If a man can control his mind he can find the way to Enlightenment, and all wisdom and virtue will naturally come to him.*
> *Buddha*

Write down all those thoughts that are weighing you down. Then let them go.
(optional; cross them out with black ink or do whatever you need to do to let them go)

Make time for peaceful activities.
An action that brought me peace today was...

_____
_____
_____
_____
_____
_____
_____
_____
_____
_____
_____

Art Therapy
Give yourself some time to scribble out those feelings. Either purposefully draw a picture or grab a color, close your eyes and let your mind go.

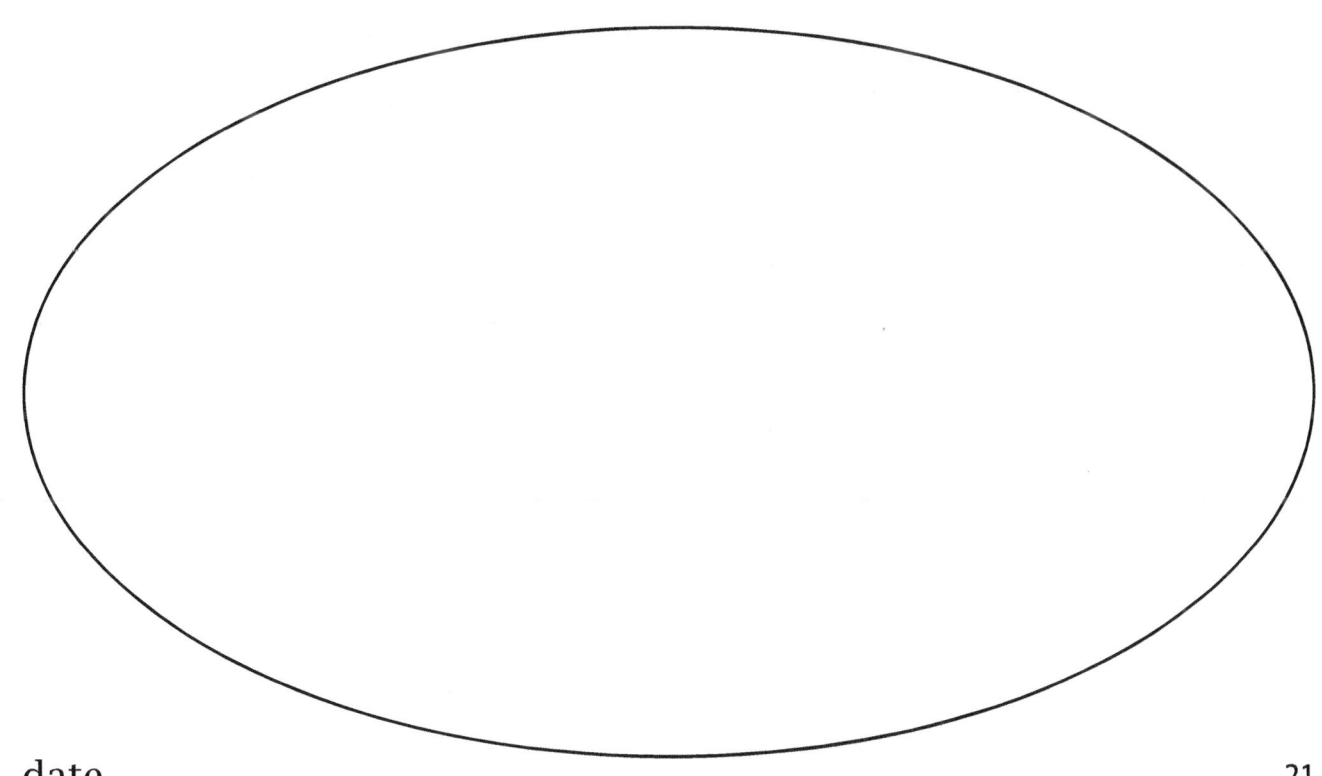

date_____

> *The Dove, on silver pinions,*
> *winged her peaceful way.*
> *James Montgomery*

Write down all those thoughts that are weighing you down. Then let them go.
(optional; cross them out with black ink or do whatever you need to do to let them go)

Make time for peaceful activities.
An action that brought me peace today was...

_____
_____
_____
_____
_____
_____
_____
_____
_____
_____

Art Therapy
Give yourself some time to scribble out those feelings. Either purposefully draw a picture or grab a color, close your eyes and let your mind go.

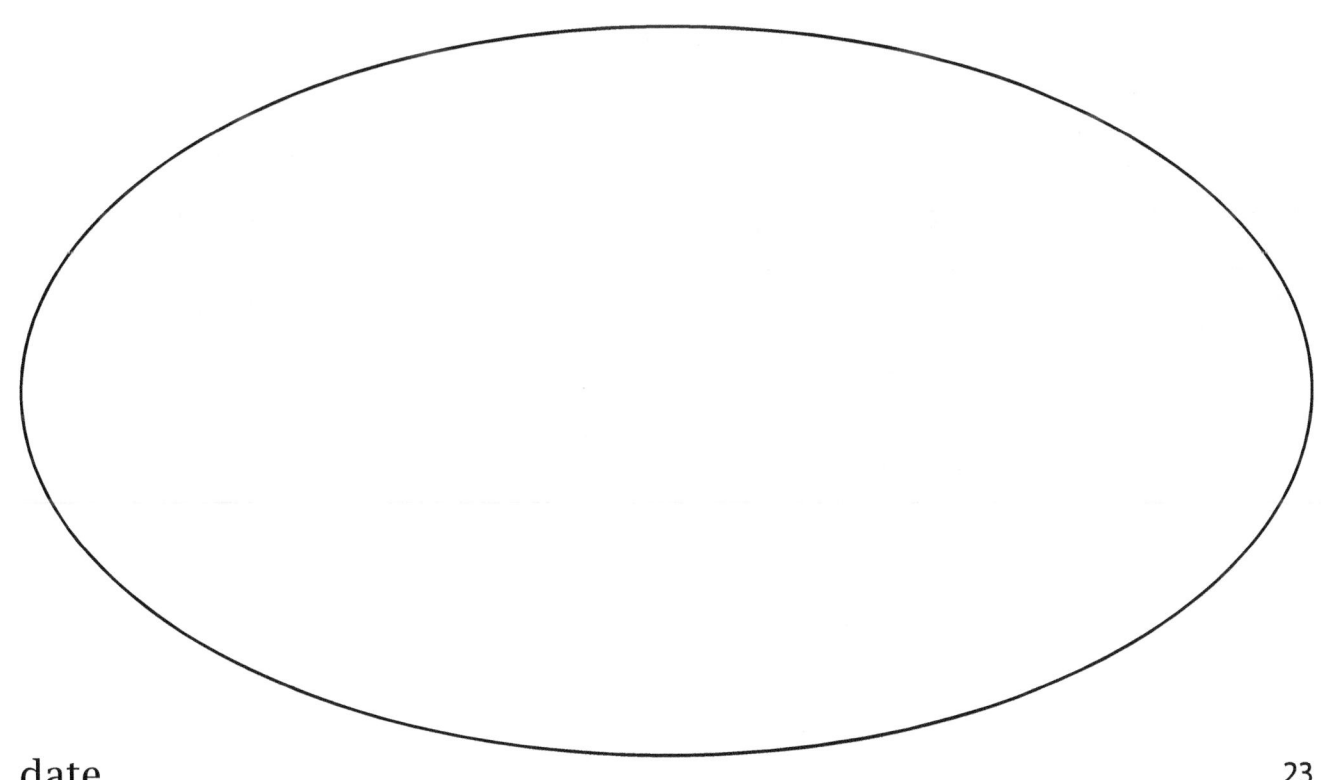

date_____

> *Imagine all the people living life in peace. You may say I'm a dreamer, but I'm not the only one. I hope someday you'll join us, and the world will be as one.*
> *John Lennon*

Write down all those thoughts that are weighing you down. Then let them go.
(optional; cross them out with black ink or do whatever you need to do to let them go)

_____
_____
_____
_____
_____
_____
_____
_____
_____
_____
_____
_____
_____
_____
_____
_____
_____
_____
_____
_____

Make time for peaceful activities.
An action that brought me peace today was...

_____
_____
_____
_____
_____
_____
_____
_____
_____
_____

Art Therapy
Give yourself some time to scribble out those feelings. Either purposefully draw a picture or grab a color, close your eyes and let your mind go.

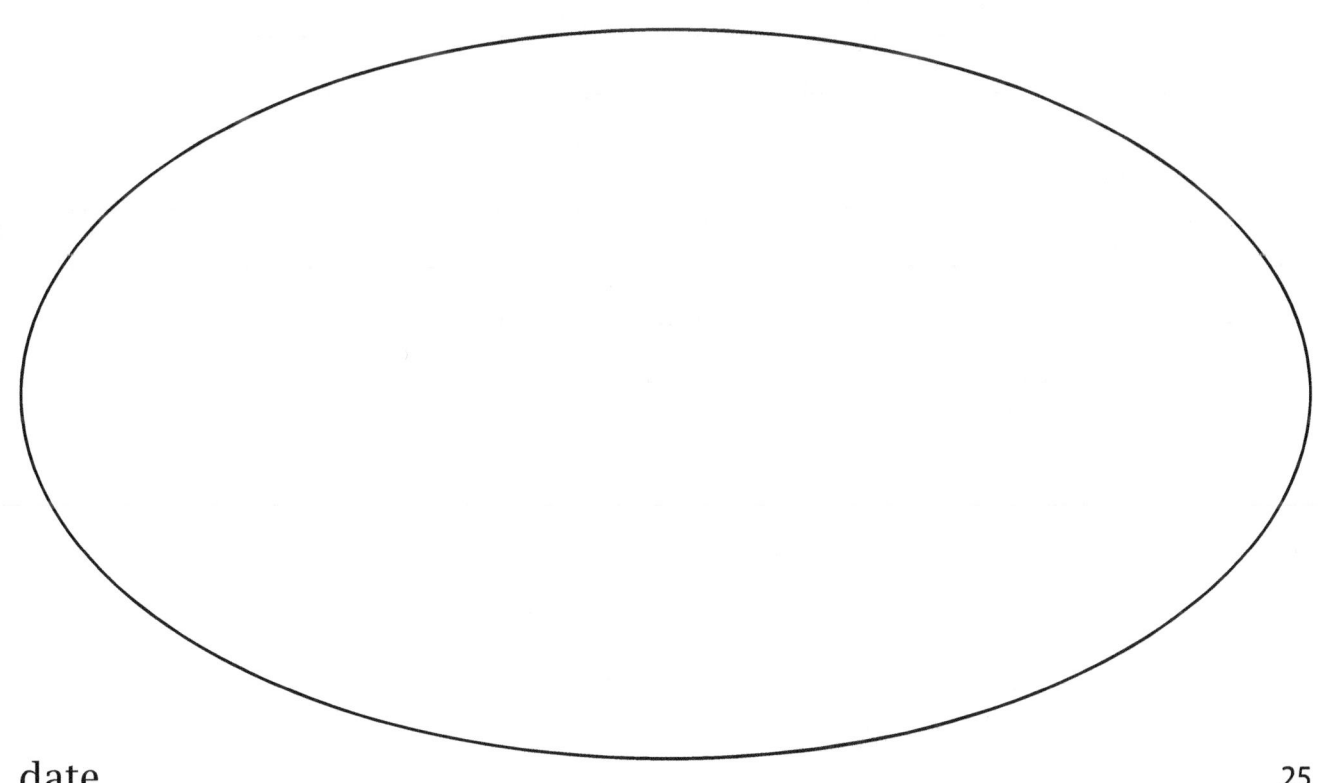

date_____

> *Never be in a hurry; do everything quietly and in a calm spirit. Do not lose your inner peace for anything whatsoever, even if your whole world seems upset.*
> *Saint Francis de Sales*

Write down all those thoughts that are weighing you down. Then let them go.
(optional; cross them out with black ink or do whatever you need to do to let them go)

Make time for peaceful activities.
An action that brought me peace today was...

_____
_____
_____
_____
_____
_____
_____
_____
_____
_____

Art Therapy
Give yourself some time to scribble out those feelings. Either purposefully draw a picture or grab a color, close your eyes and let your mind go.

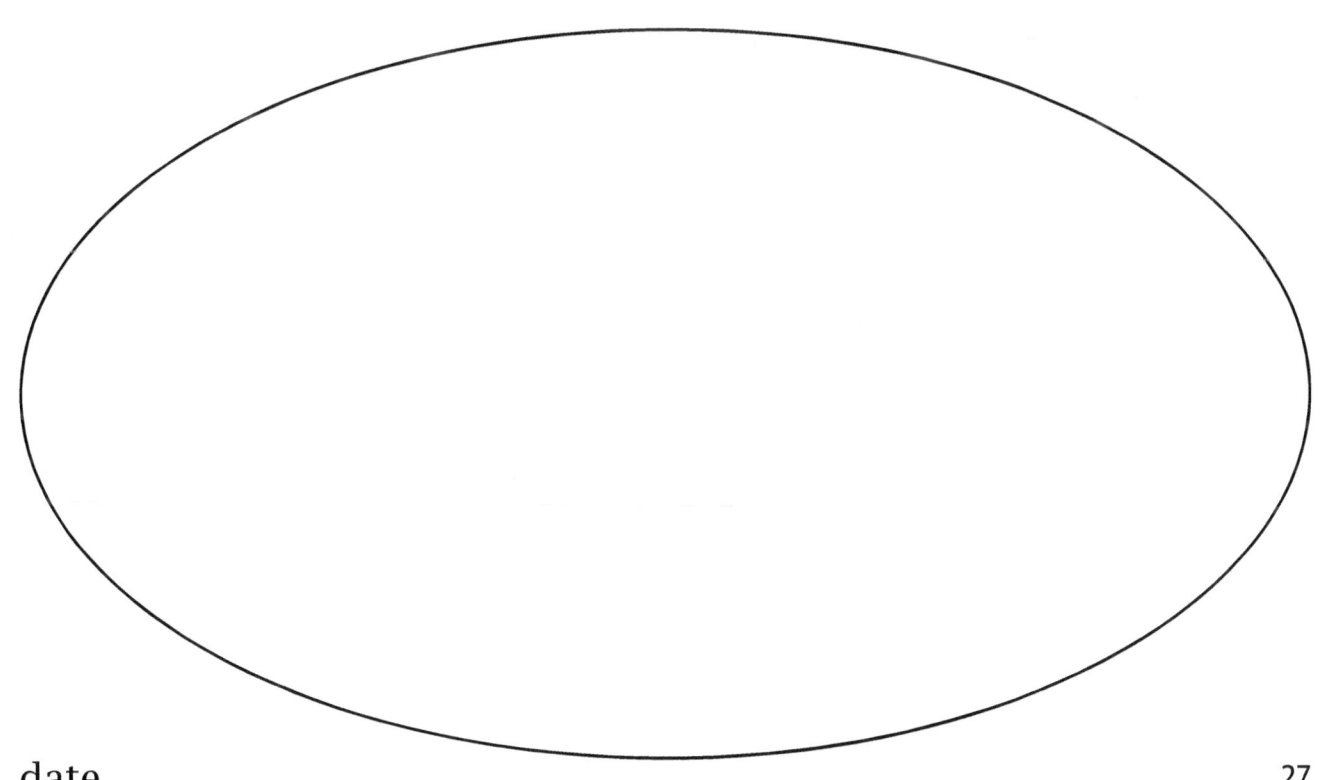

date_____

> *If your mind is at peace, you are happy. If your mind is at peace, but you have nothing else, you can be happy. If you have everything the world can give - pleasure, possessions, power - but lack peace of mind, you can never be happy.*
> *Dada Vaswani*

Write down all those thoughts that are weighing you down. Then let them go.
(optional; cross them out with black ink or do whatever you need to do to let them go)

_____
_____
_____
_____
_____
_____
_____
_____
_____
_____
_____
_____
_____
_____
_____
_____
_____
_____

Make time for peaceful activities.
An action that brought me peace today was...

_____
_____
_____
_____
_____
_____
_____
_____
_____
_____

Art Therapy
Give yourself some time to scribble out those feelings. Either purposefully draw a picture or grab a color, close your eyes and let your mind go.

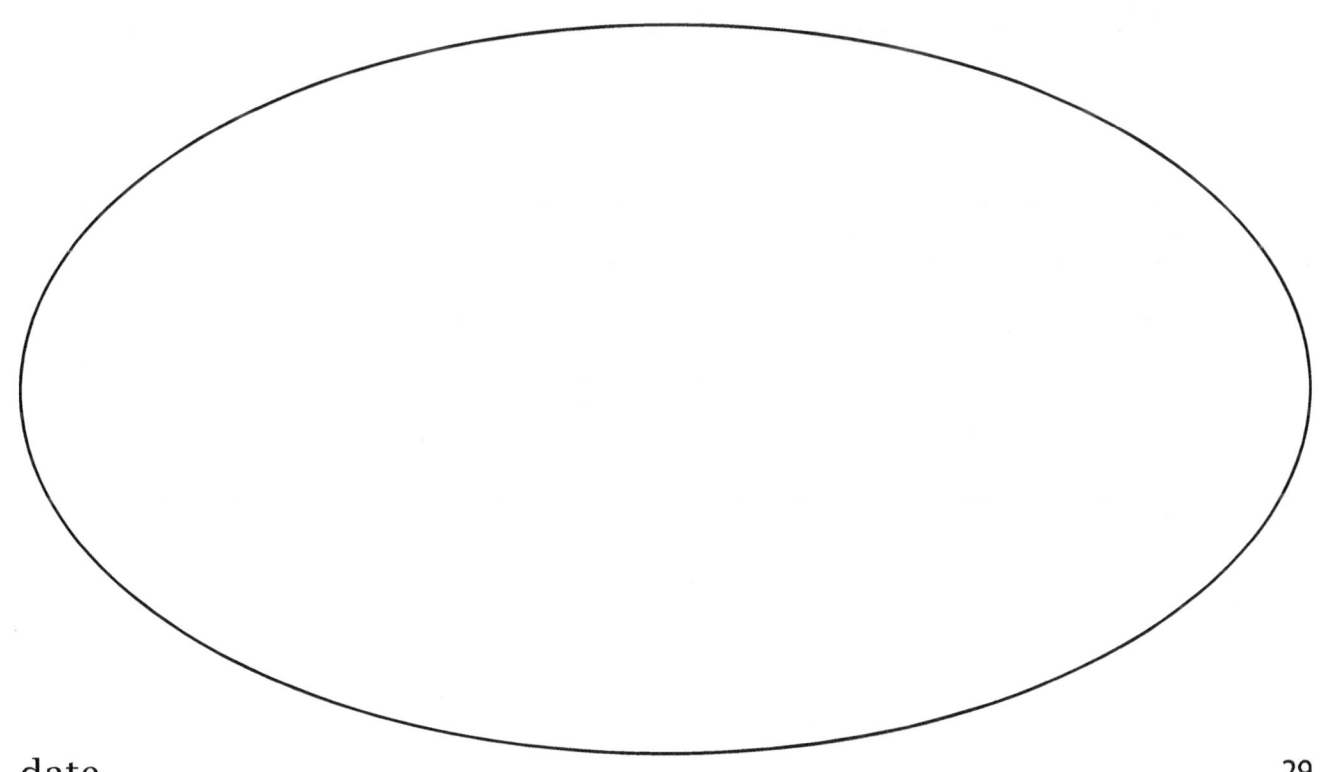

date_____

> *If we have no peace, it is because we have forgotten that we belong to each other.*
> *Mother Teresa*

Write down all those thoughts that are weighing you down. Then let them go.
(optional; cross them out with black ink or do whatever you need to do to let them go)

Make time for peaceful activities.
An action that brought me peace today was...

_____
_____
_____
_____
_____
_____
_____
_____
_____

Art Therapy
Give yourself some time to scribble out those feelings. Either purposefully draw a picture or grab a color, close your eyes and let your mind go.

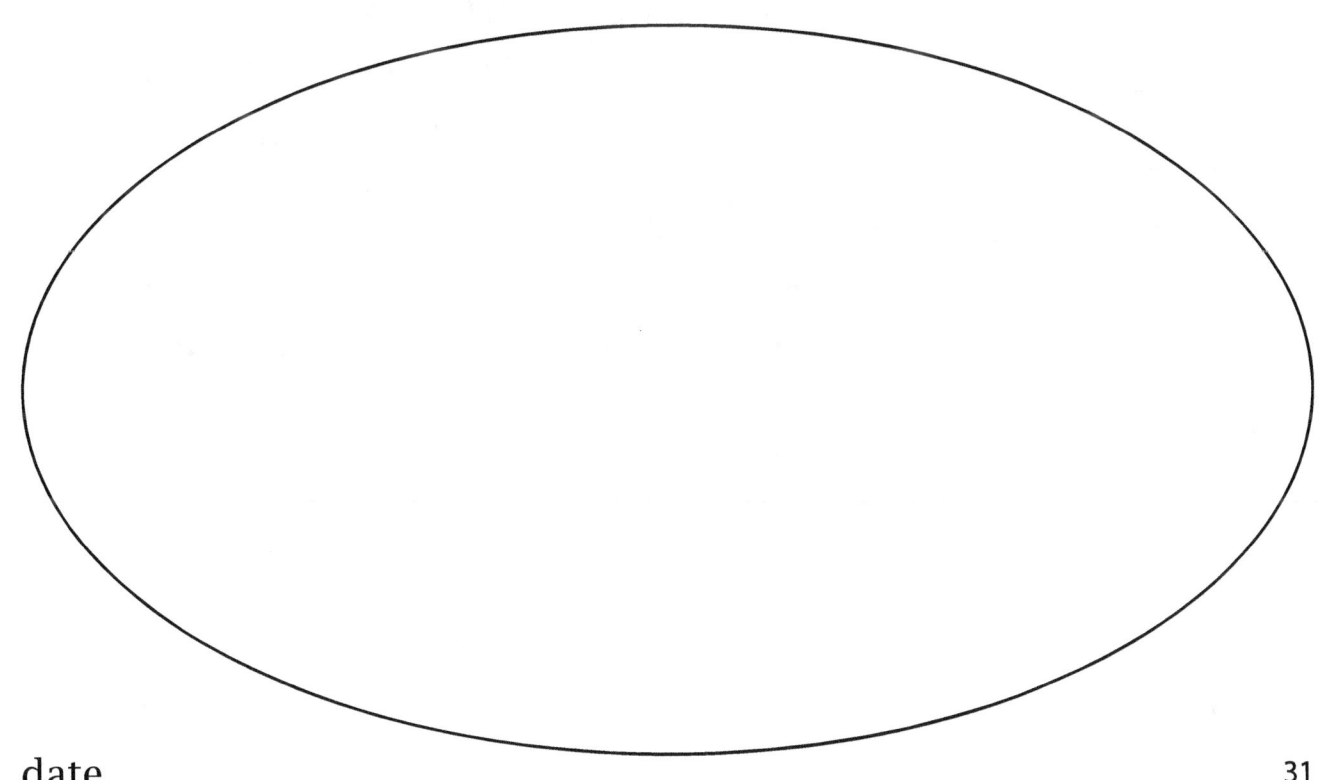

date_____

What a week! I love my peaceful journal.

Write down the difference you notice in your life as you have been focused on peace.

_____
_____
_____
_____
_____
_____
_____
_____
_____

> *We can never obtain peace in the outer world until we make peace with ourselves.*
> *Dalai Lama*

**** *My daily peaceful actions* ****

_____
_____
_____
_____

Dear _____

I have something I need to tell you. I forgive you for...

_____
_____
_____
_____
_____
_____
_____
_____
_____
_____
_____
_____
_____
_____
_____
_____
_____
_____
_____
_____

peaceful meter

| I think I am going to scream | | I am like a cloud floating on a breeze |

> *First keep peace with yourself, then you can also bring peace to others.*
> *Thomas a Kempis*

Write down all those thoughts that are weighing you down. Then let them go.
(optional; cross them out with black ink or do whatever you need to do to let them go)

Make time for peaceful activities.
An action that brought me peace today was...

_____
_____
_____
_____
_____
_____
_____
_____
_____
_____

Art Therapy
Give yourself some time to scribble out those feelings. Either purposefully draw a picture or grab a color, close your eyes and let your mind go.

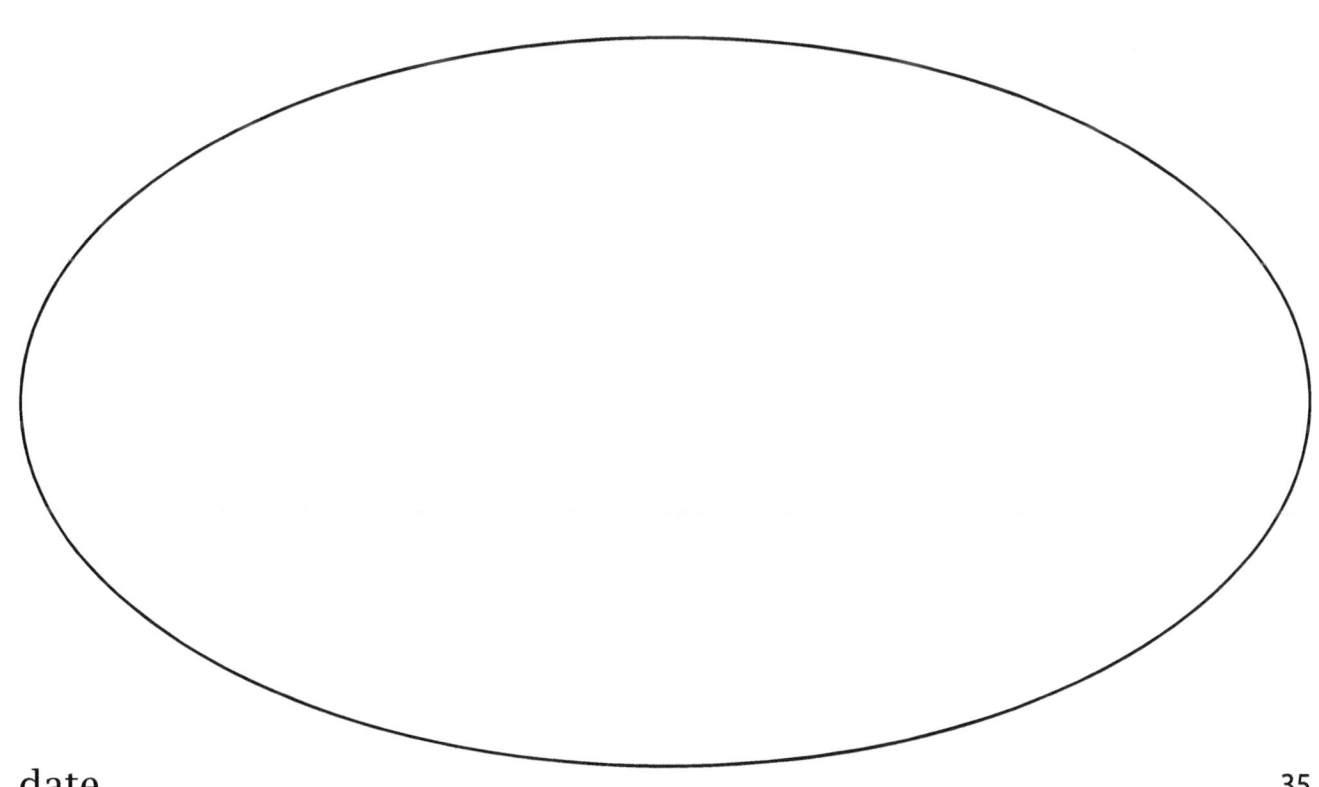

date_____

> *It isn't enough to talk about peace. One must believe in it. And it isn't enough to believe in it. One must work at it.*
> *Eleanor Roosevelt*

Write down all those thoughts that are weighing you down. Then let them go.
(optional; cross them out with black ink or do whatever you need to do to let them go)

Make time for peaceful activities.
An action that brought me peace today was...

_____
_____
_____
_____
_____
_____
_____
_____
_____
_____

Art Therapy
Give yourself some time to scribble out those feelings. Either purposefully draw a picture or grab a color, close your eyes and let your mind go.

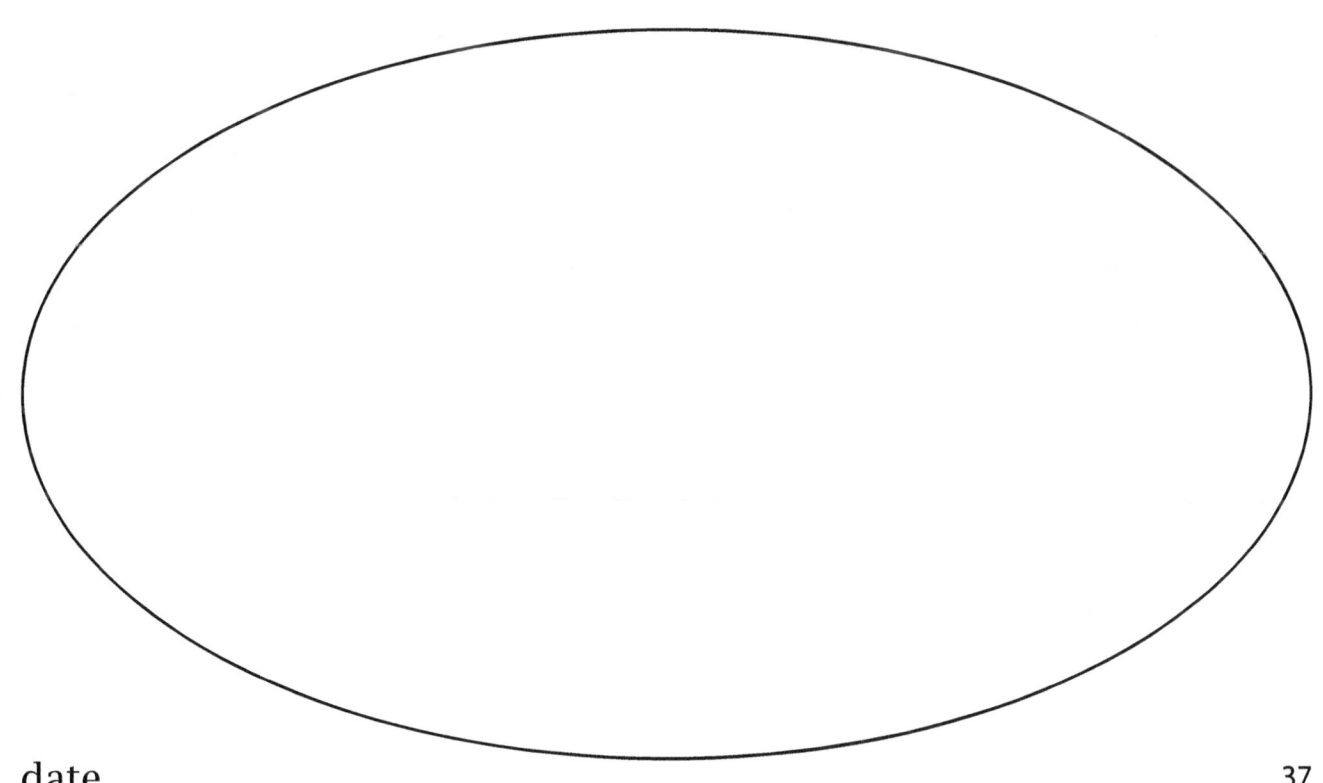

date_____

> *I'm concentrating on staying healthy, having peace, being happy, remembering what is important, taking in nature and animals, spending time reading, trying to understand the universe, where science and the spiritual meet.*
> *Joan Jett*

Write down all those thoughts that are weighing you down. Then let them go.
(optional; cross them out with black ink or do whatever you need to do to let them go)

Make time for peaceful activities.
An action that brought me peace today was...

_____
_____
_____
_____
_____
_____
_____
_____
_____
_____

Art Therapy
Give yourself some time to scribble out those feelings. Either purposefully draw a picture or grab a color, close your eyes and let your mind go.

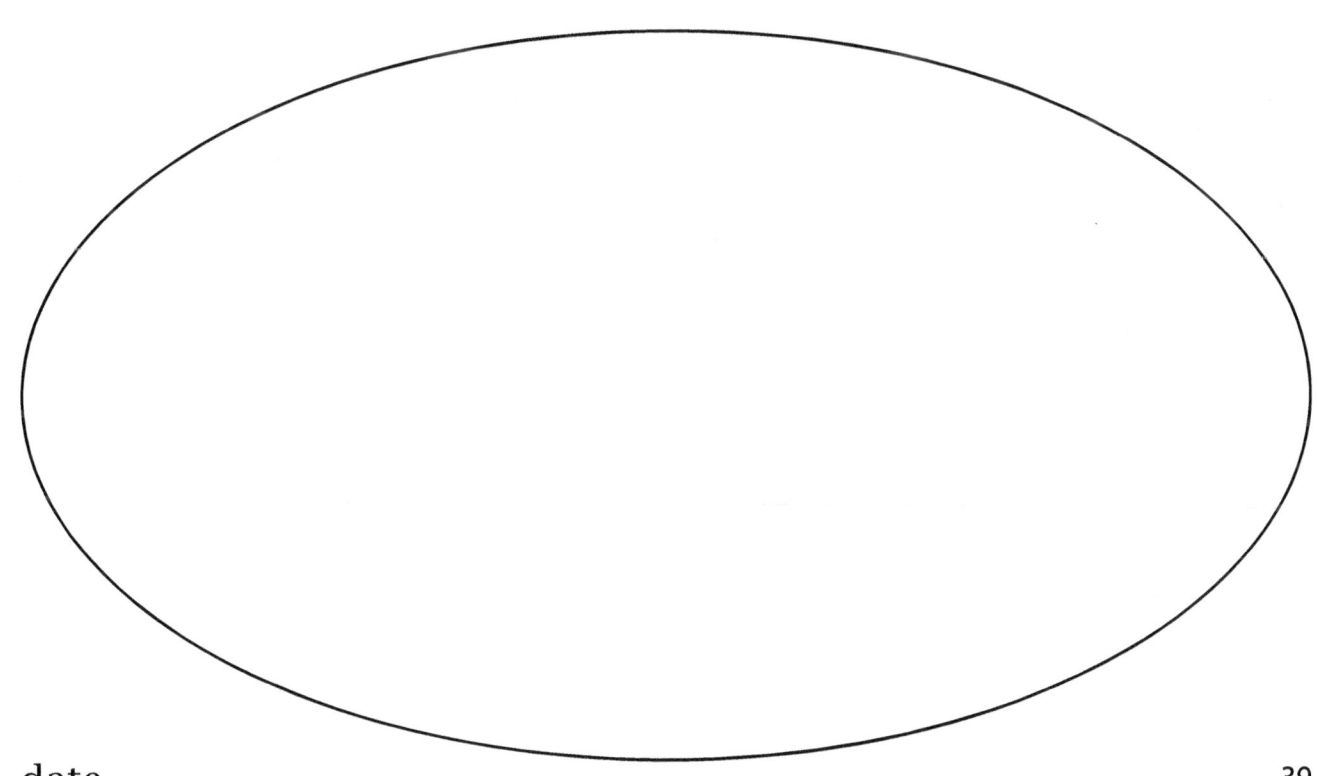

date_____

> *Nobody can bring you peace but yourself.*
> *Ralph Waldo Emerson*

Write down all those thoughts that are weighing you down. Then let them go.
(optional; cross them out with black ink or do whatever you need to do to let them go)

Make time for peaceful activities.
An action that brought me peace today was...

_____
_____
_____
_____
_____
_____
_____
_____
_____

Art Therapy
Give yourself some time to scribble out those feelings. Either purposefully draw a picture or grab a color, close your eyes and let your mind go.

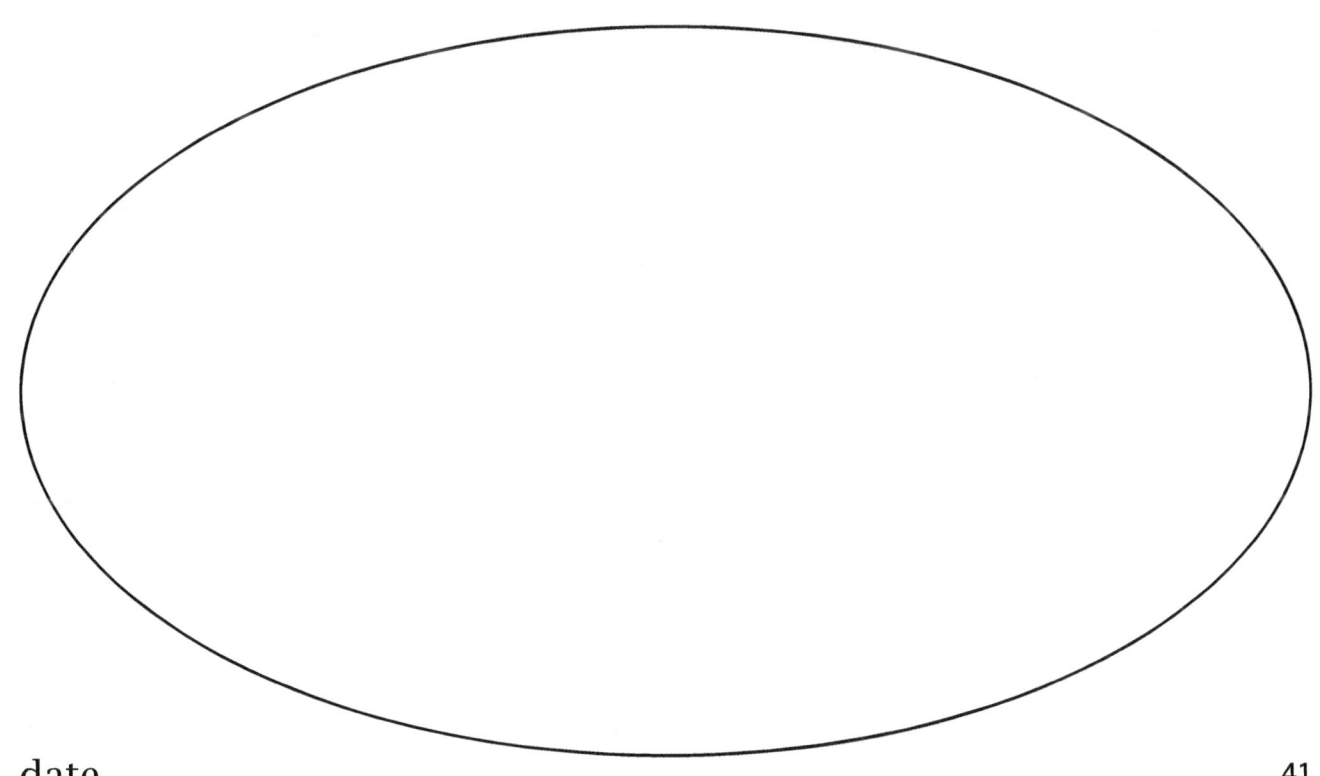

date_____

> *All we are saying is give peace a chance.*
> *John Lennon*

Write down all those thoughts that are weighing you down. Then let them go.
(optional; cross them out with black ink or do whatever you need to do to let them go)

Make time for peaceful activities.
An action that brought me peace today was...

_____
_____
_____
_____
_____
_____
_____
_____
_____
_____

Art Therapy
Give yourself some time to scribble out those feelings. Either purposefully draw a picture or grab a color, close your eyes and let your mind go.

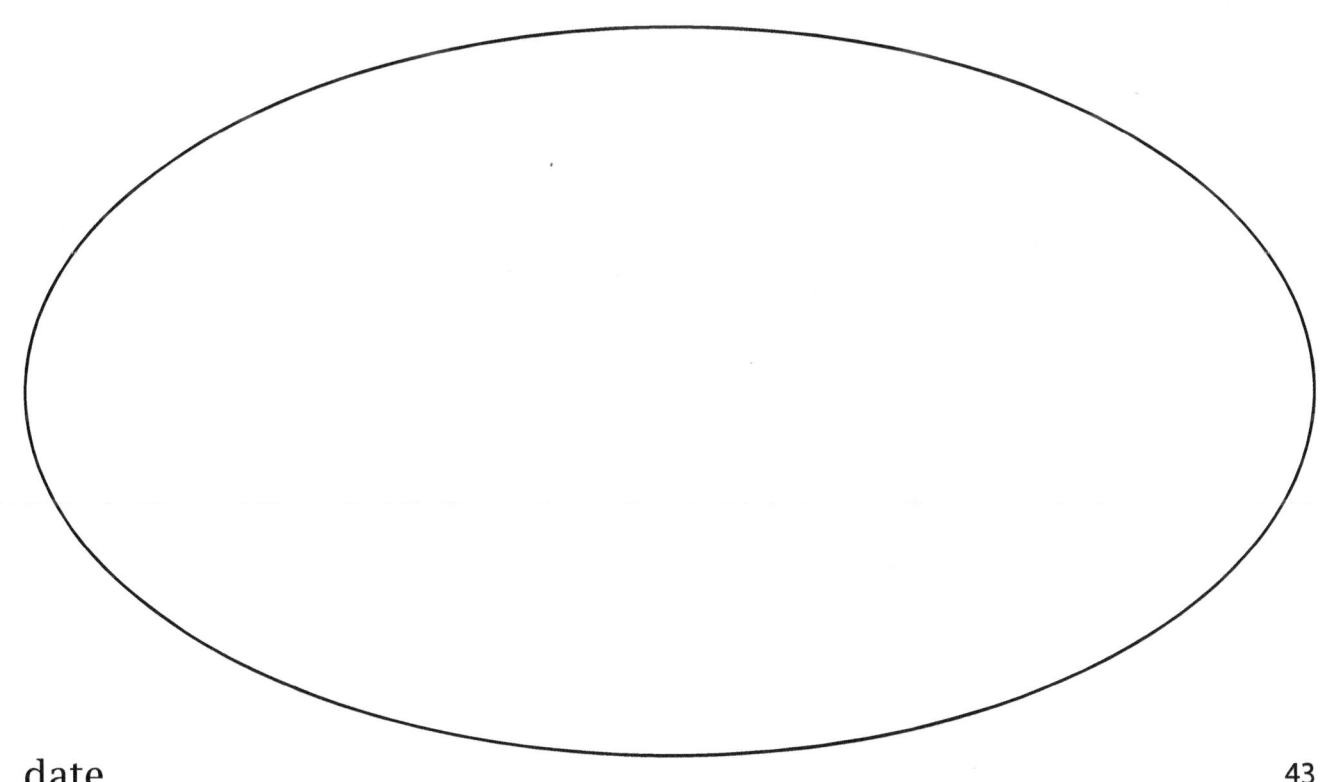

date_____

> *I took a deep breath and listened*
> *to the old bray of my heart.*
> *I am. I am. I am.*
> *Sylvia Plath*

Write down all those thoughts that are weighing you down. Then let them go.
(optional; cross them out with black ink or do whatever you need to do to let them go)

Make time for peaceful activities.
An action that brought me peace today was...

_____
_____
_____
_____
_____
_____
_____
_____
_____

Art Therapy
Give yourself some time to scribble out those feelings. Either purposefully draw a picture or grab a color, close your eyes and let your mind go.

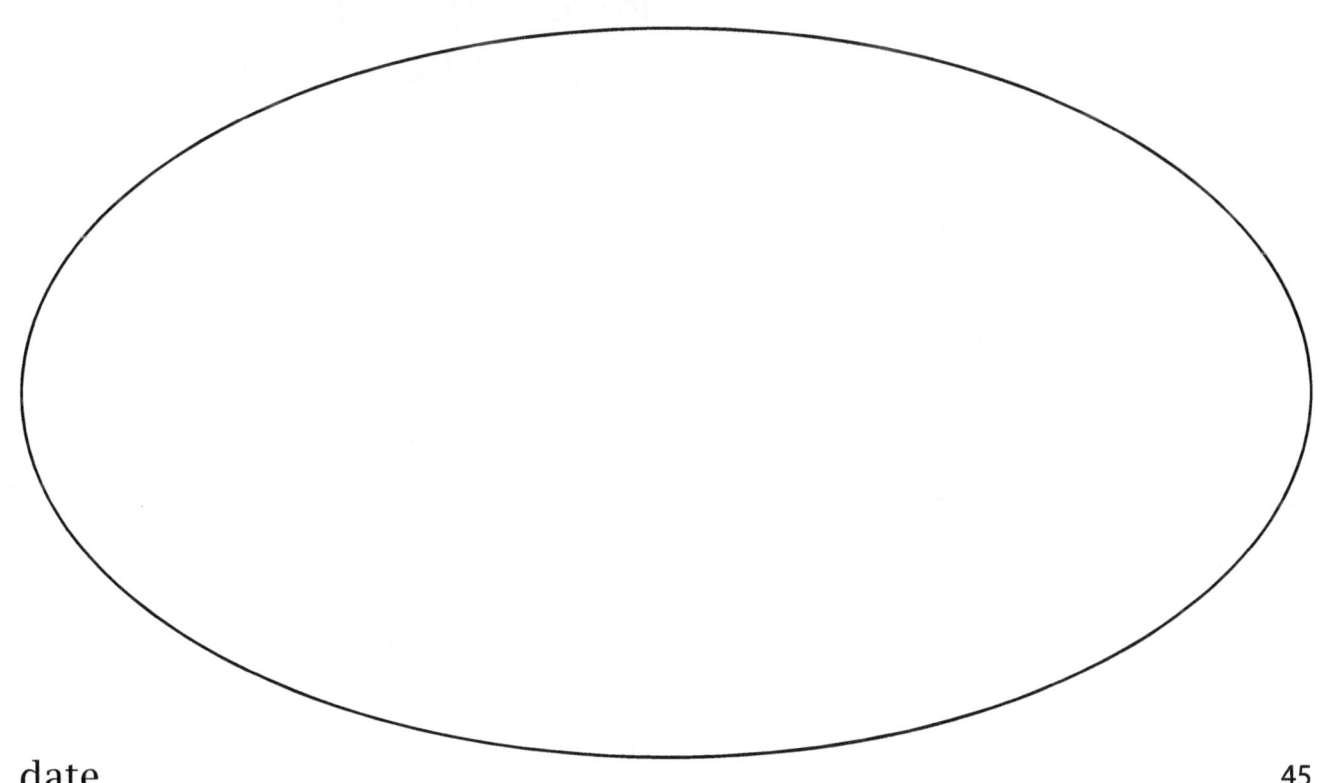

date_____

What a week! I love my peaceful journal.

Write down the difference you notice in your life as you have been focused on peace.

Peace begins with a smile.
Mother Teresa

**** My daily peaceful actions ****

Dear _____

I have something I need to tell you. I forgive you for...

_____
_____
_____
_____
_____
_____
_____
_____
_____
_____
_____
_____
_____
_____
_____
_____
_____
_____
_____
_____

peaceful meter

| I think I am going to scream | | I am like a cloud floating on a breeze |

> *Better than a thousand hollow words, is one word that brings peace.*
> *Buddha*

Write down all those thoughts that are weighing you down. Then let them go.
(optional; cross them out with black ink or do whatever you need to do to let them go)

Make time for peaceful activities.
An action that brought me peace today was...

_____
_____
_____
_____
_____
_____
_____
_____
_____
_____

Art Therapy
Give yourself some time to scribble out those feelings. Either purposefully draw a picture or grab a color, close your eyes and let your mind go.

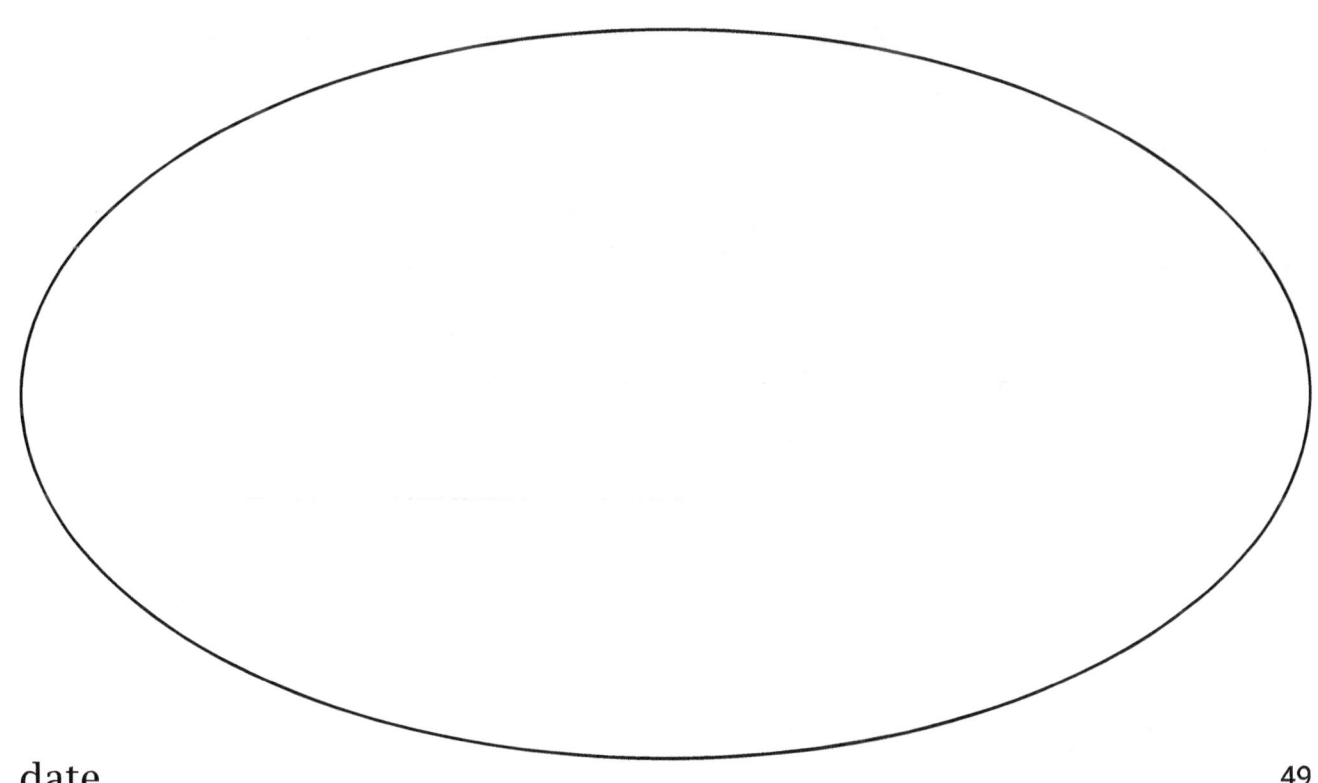

date_____

> *You cannot find peace by avoiding life.*
> *Virginia Woolf*

Write down all those thoughts that are weighing you down. Then let them go.
(optional; cross them out with black ink or do whatever you need to do to let them go)

Make time for peaceful activities.
An action that brought me peace today was...

_____
_____
_____
_____
_____
_____
_____
_____
_____

Art Therapy
Give yourself some time to scribble out those feelings. Either purposefully draw a picture or grab a color, close your eyes and let your mind go.

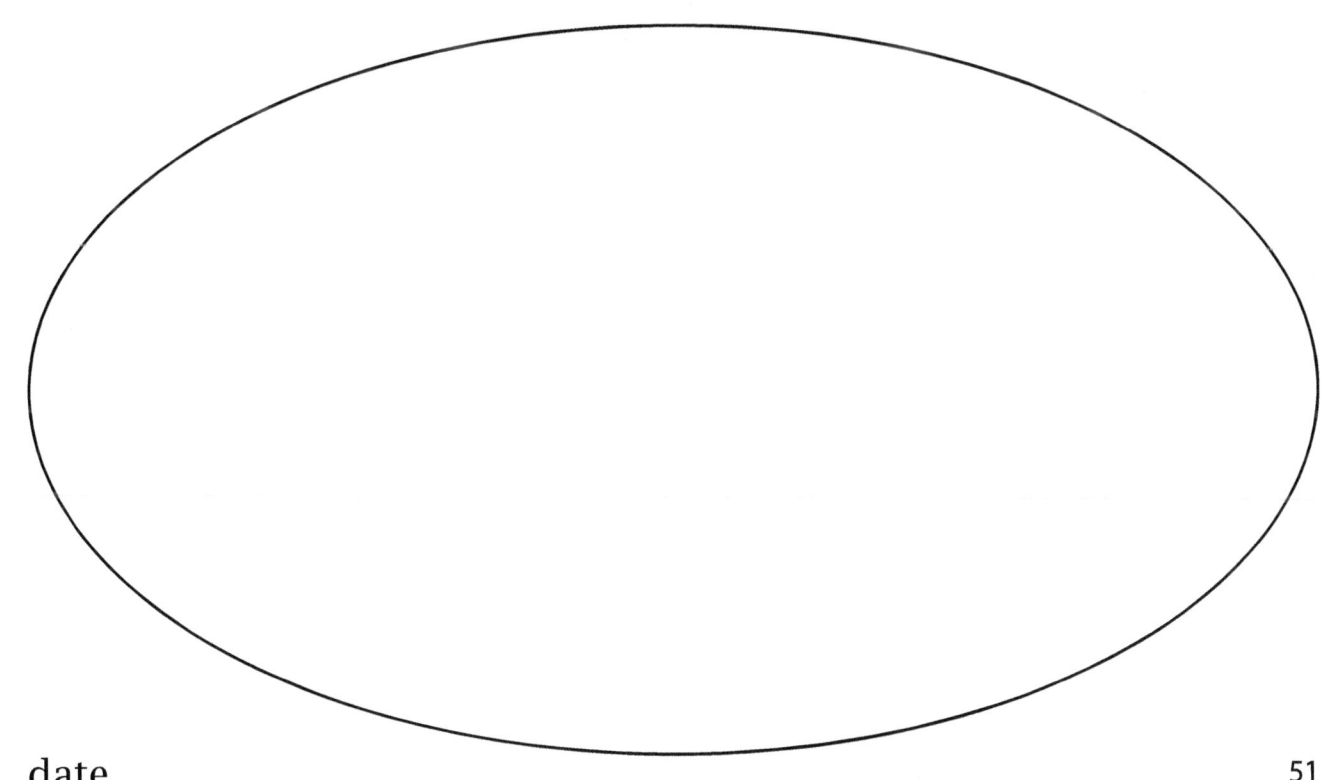

date_____

> *He that would live in peace and at ease must not speak all he knows or all he sees.*
> *Benjamin Franklin*

Write down all those thoughts that are weighing you down. Then let them go.
(optional; cross them out with black ink or do whatever you need to do to let them go)

_____
_____
_____
_____
_____
_____
_____
_____
_____
_____
_____
_____
_____
_____
_____
_____
_____
_____
_____

Make time for peaceful activities.
An action that brought me peace today was...

_____
_____
_____
_____
_____
_____
_____
_____
_____
_____

Art Therapy
Give yourself some time to scribble out those feelings. Either purposefully draw a picture or grab a color, close your eyes and let your mind go.

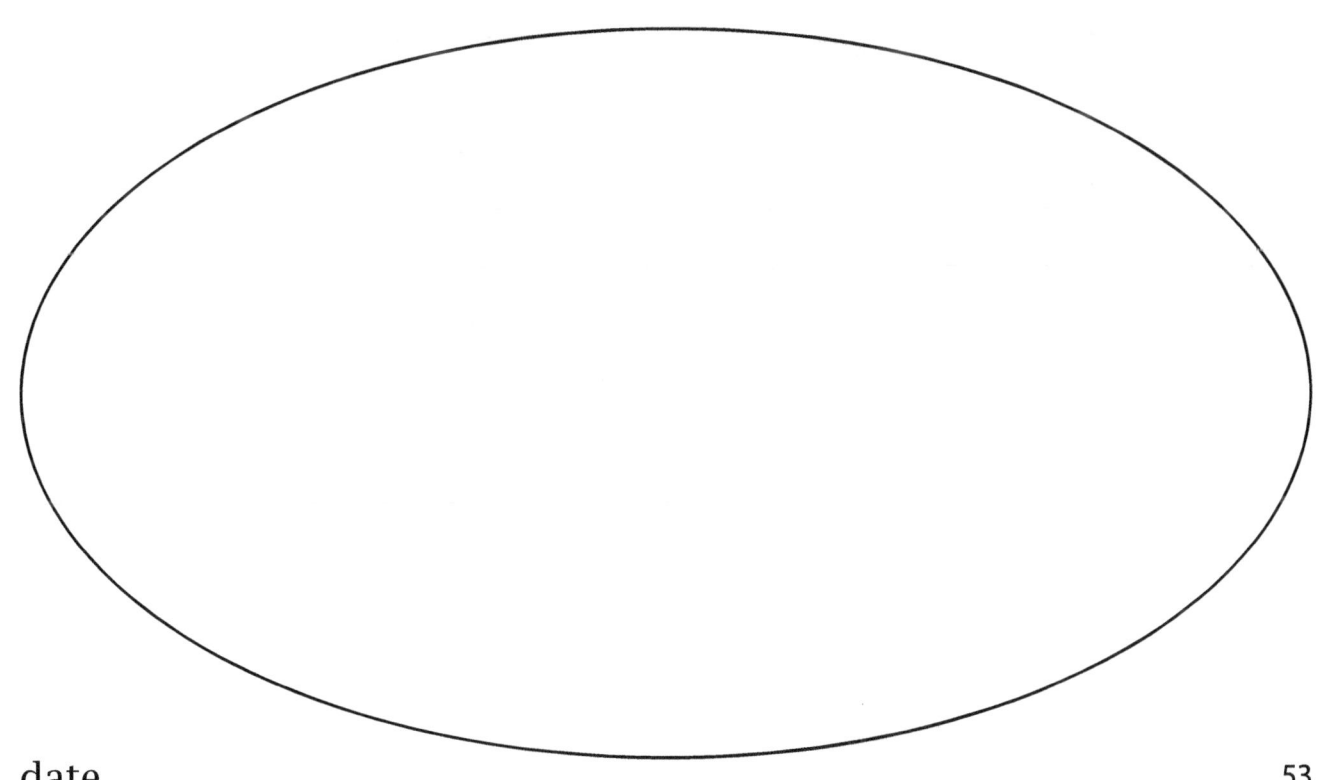

date_____

> *Peace is liberty in tranquility.*
> *Marcus Tullius Cicero*

Write down all those thoughts that are weighing you down. Then let them go.
(optional; cross them out with black ink or do whatever you need to do to let them go)

_____
_____
_____
_____
_____
_____
_____
_____
_____
_____
_____
_____
_____
_____
_____
_____
_____
_____
_____

Make time for peaceful activities.
An action that brought me peace today was...

_____
_____
_____
_____
_____
_____
_____
_____
_____
_____

Art Therapy
Give yourself some time to scribble out those feelings. Either purposefully draw a picture or grab a color, close your eyes and let your mind go.

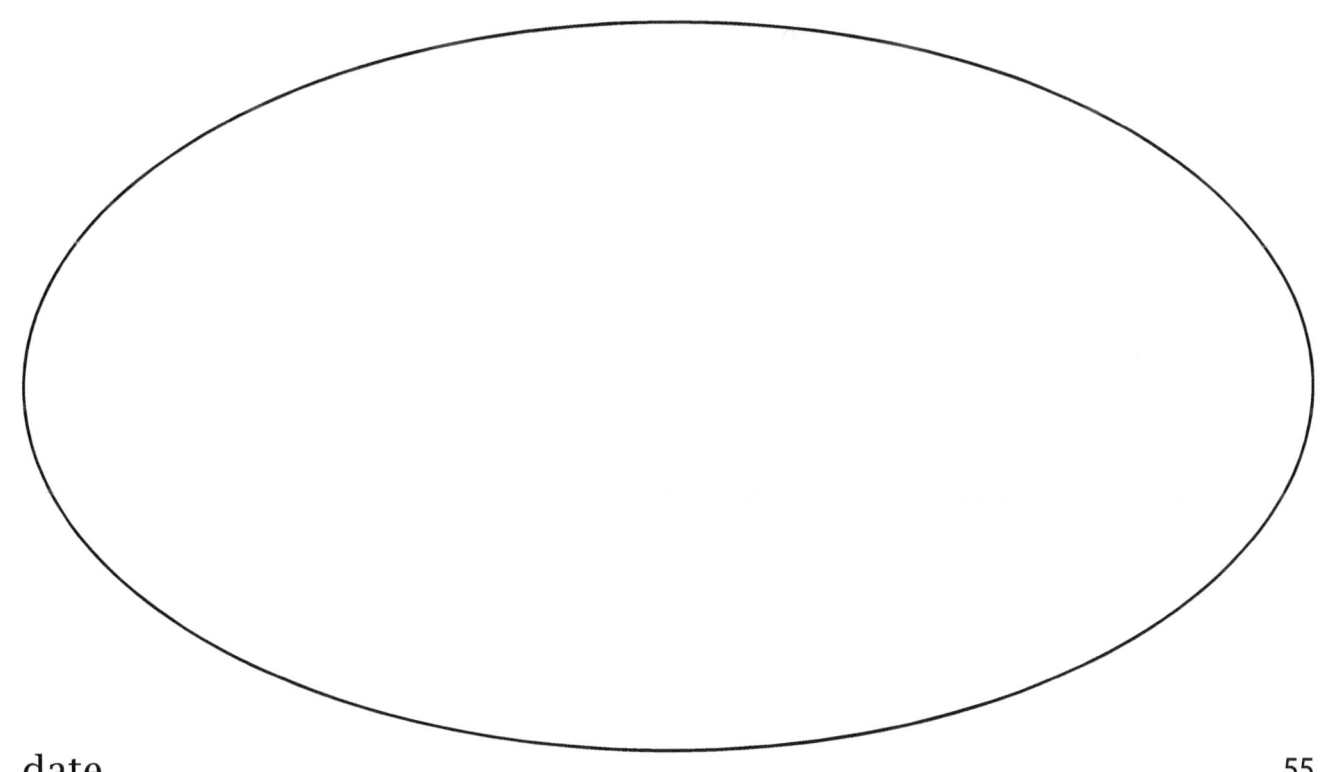

date_____

> *Peace is a daily, a weekly, a monthly process, gradually changing opinions, slowly eroding old barriers, quietly building new structures.*
> *John F. Kennedy*

Write down all those thoughts that are weighing you down. Then let them go.

(optional; cross them out with black ink or do whatever you need to do to let them go)

_____
_____
_____
_____
_____
_____
_____
_____
_____
_____
_____
_____
_____
_____
_____
_____
_____
_____
_____
_____

Make time for peaceful activities.
An action that brought me peace today was...

_____
_____
_____
_____
_____
_____
_____
_____
_____
_____

Art Therapy
Give yourself some time to scribble out those feelings. Either purposefully draw a picture or grab a color, close your eyes and let your mind go.

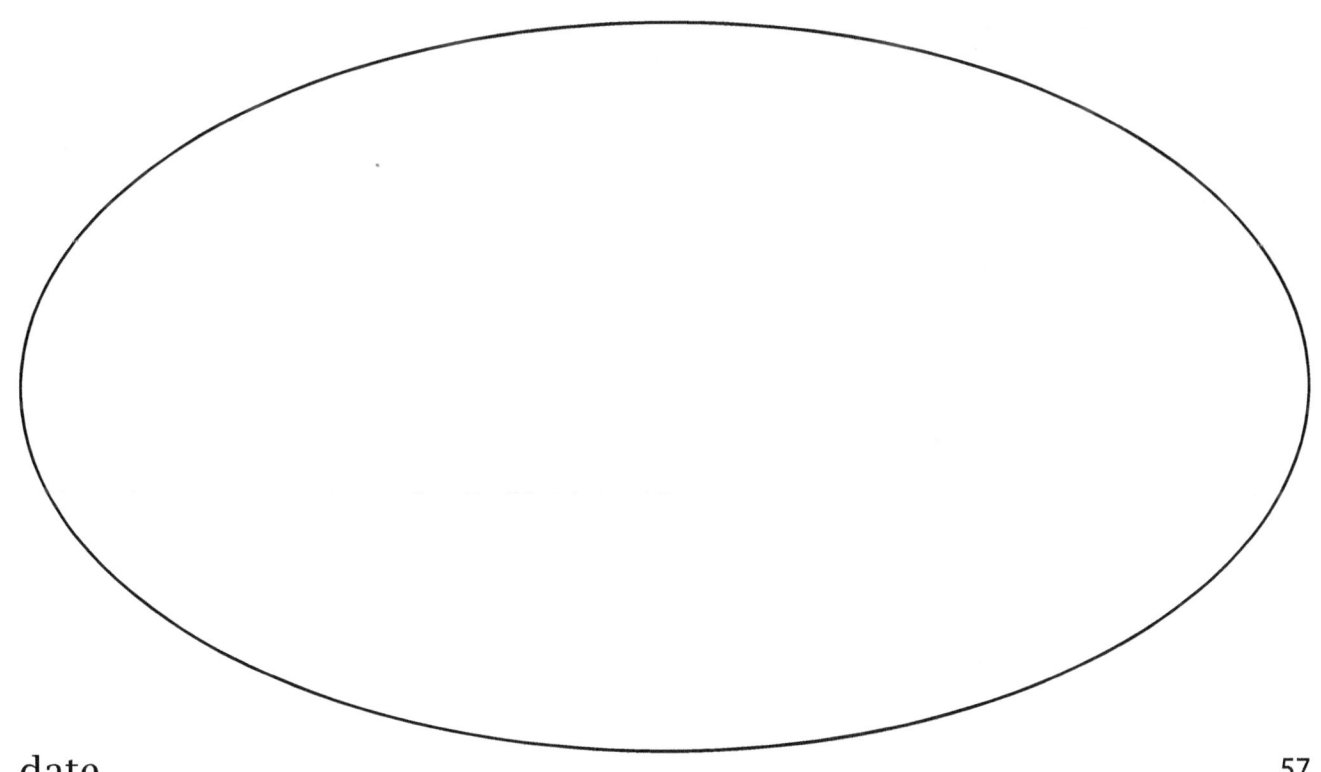

date_____

> *While you are proclaiming peace with your lips, be careful to have it even more fully in your heart.*
> *Francis of Assisi*

Write down all those thoughts that are weighing you down. Then let them go.
(optional; cross them out with black ink or do whatever you need to do to let them go)

Make time for peaceful activities.
An action that brought me peace today was...

_____
_____
_____
_____
_____
_____
_____
_____
_____
_____

Art Therapy
Give yourself some time to scribble out those feelings. Either purposefully draw a picture or grab a color, close your eyes and let your mind go.

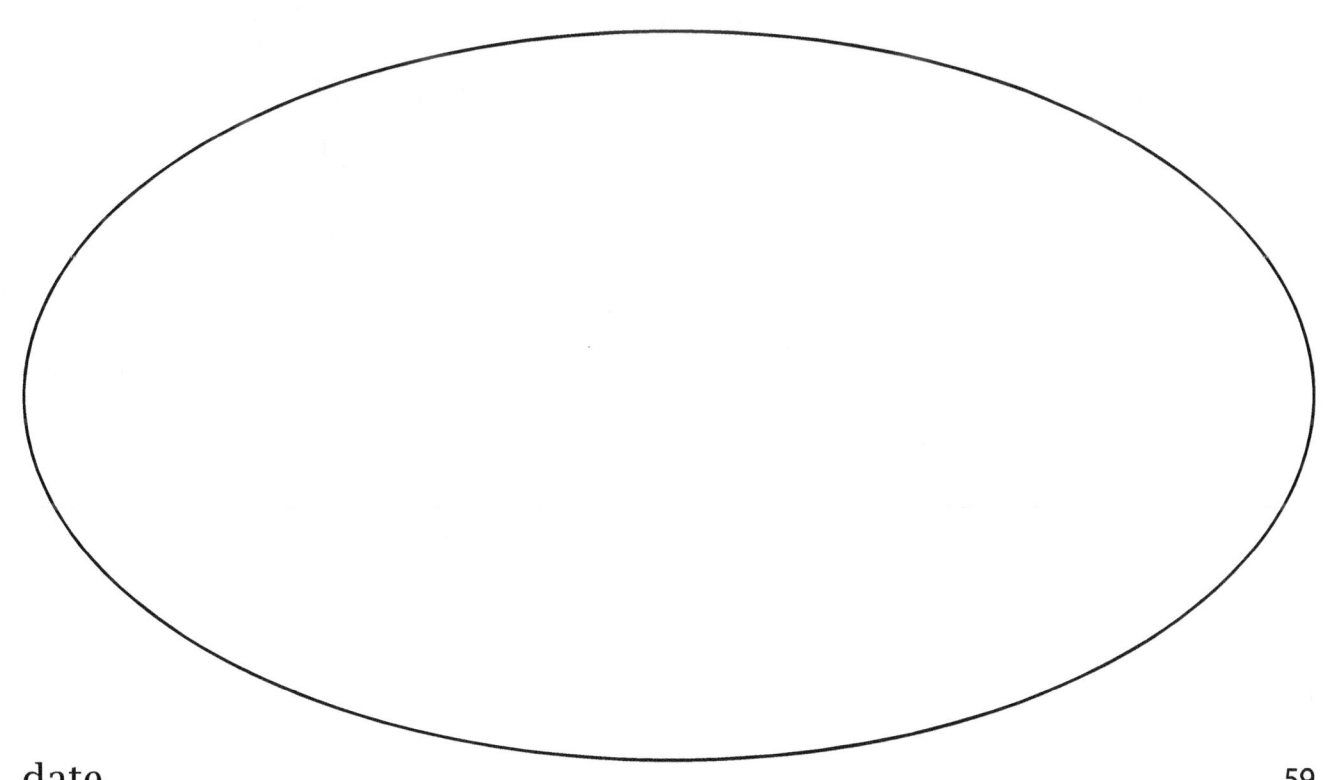

date_____

What a week! I love my peaceful journal.

Write down the difference you notice in your life as you have been focused on peace.

_____
_____
_____
_____
_____
_____
_____
_____
_____
_____
_____
_____
_____
_____
_____

> *Those who are free of resentful thoughts surely find peace.*
> *Buddha*

**** *My daily peaceful actions* ****

_____
_____
_____
_____

Dear _____

I have something I need to tell you. I forgive you for...

_____
_____
_____
_____
_____
_____
_____
_____
_____
_____
_____
_____
_____
_____
_____
_____
_____
_____
_____

peaceful meter

I think I am going to scream — I am like a cloud floating on a breeze

> *The pursuit, even of the best things,*
> *ought to be calm and tranquil.*
> *Marcus Tullius Cicero*

Write down all those thoughts that are weighing you down. Then let them go.
(optional; cross them out with black ink or do whatever you need to do to let them go)

Make time for peaceful activities.
An action that brought me peace today was...

_____
_____
_____
_____
_____
_____
_____
_____
_____
_____

Art Therapy
Give yourself some time to scribble out those feelings. Either purposefully draw a picture or grab a color, close your eyes and let your mind go.

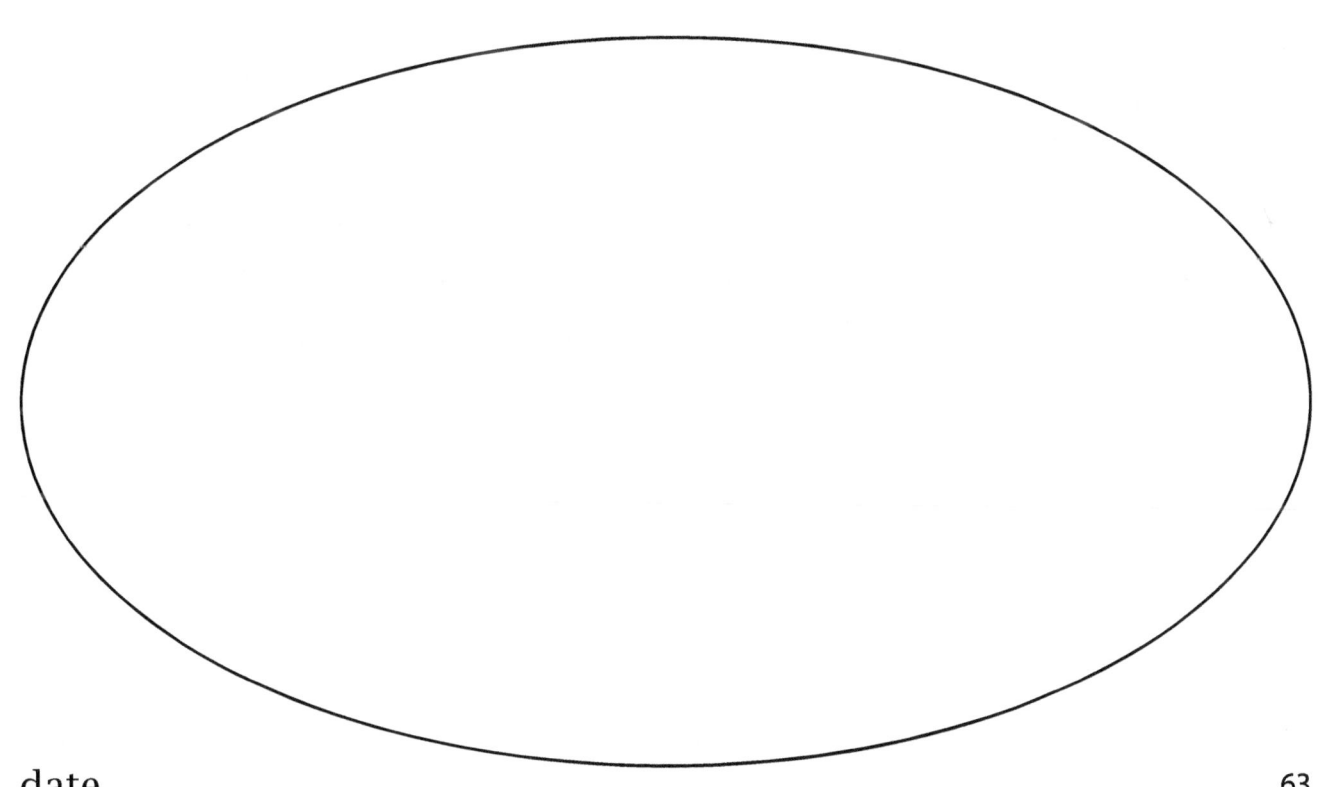

date_____

> *Each one has to find his peace from within.*
> *And peace to be real must be unaffected by*
> *outside circumstances.*
> *Mahatma Gandhi*

Write down all those thoughts that are weighing you down. Then let them go.
(optional; cross them out with black ink or do whatever you need to do to let them go)

___
___
___
___
___
___
___
___
___
___
___
___
___
___
___
___
___
___
___
___
___

Make time for peaceful activities.
An action that brought me peace today was...

_____
_____
_____
_____
_____
_____
_____
_____
_____
_____

Art Therapy
Give yourself some time to scribble out those feelings. Either purposefully draw a picture or grab a color, close your eyes and let your mind go.

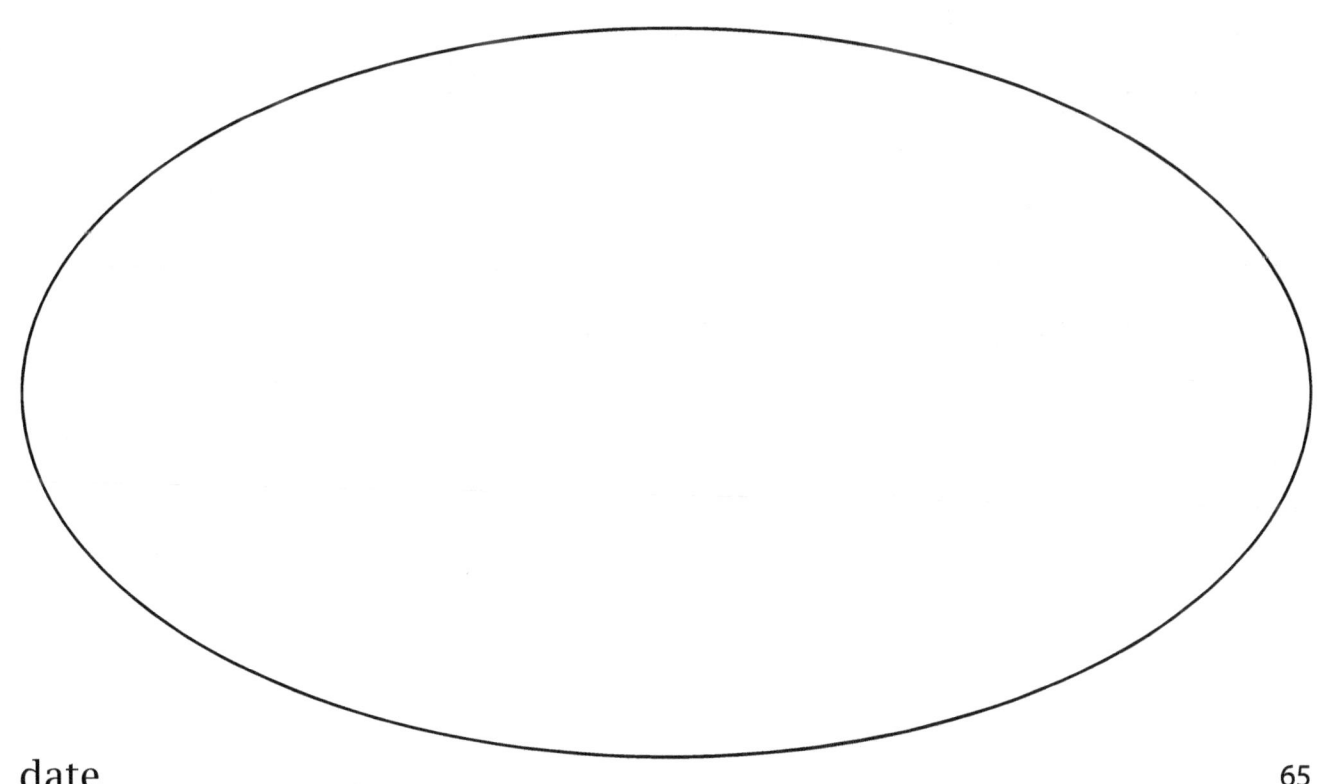

date_____

> *If everyone demanded peace instead of another television set, then there'd be peace.*
> *John Lennon*

Write down all those thoughts that are weighing you down. Then let them go.
(optional; cross them out with black ink or do whatever you need to do to let them go)

Make time for peaceful activities.
An action that brought me peace today was...

_____
_____
_____
_____
_____
_____
_____
_____
_____
_____

Art Therapy
Give yourself some time to scribble out those feelings. Either purposefully draw a picture or grab a color, close your eyes and let your mind go.

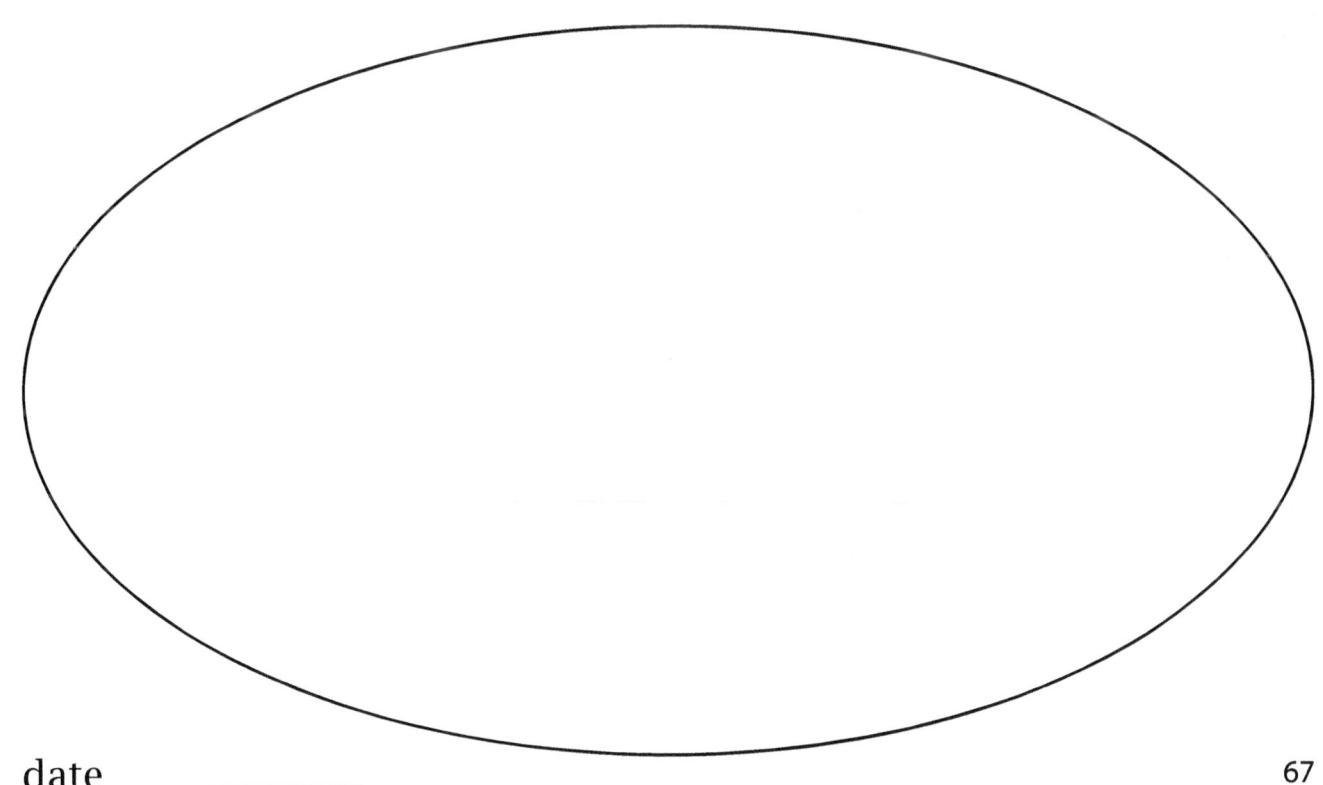

date_____

> *The simplification of life is one of the steps to inner peace. A persistent simplification will create an inner and outer well-being that places harmony in one's life.*
> *Peace Pilgrim*

Write down all those thoughts that are weighing you down. Then let them go.
(optional; cross them out with black ink or do whatever you need to do to let them go)

_____
_____
_____
_____
_____
_____
_____
_____
_____
_____
_____
_____
_____
_____
_____
_____
_____
_____
_____
_____

Make time for peaceful activities.
An action that brought me peace today was...

_____
_____
_____
_____
_____
_____
_____
_____
_____

Art Therapy
Give yourself some time to scribble out those feelings. Either purposefully draw a picture or grab a color, close your eyes and let your mind go.

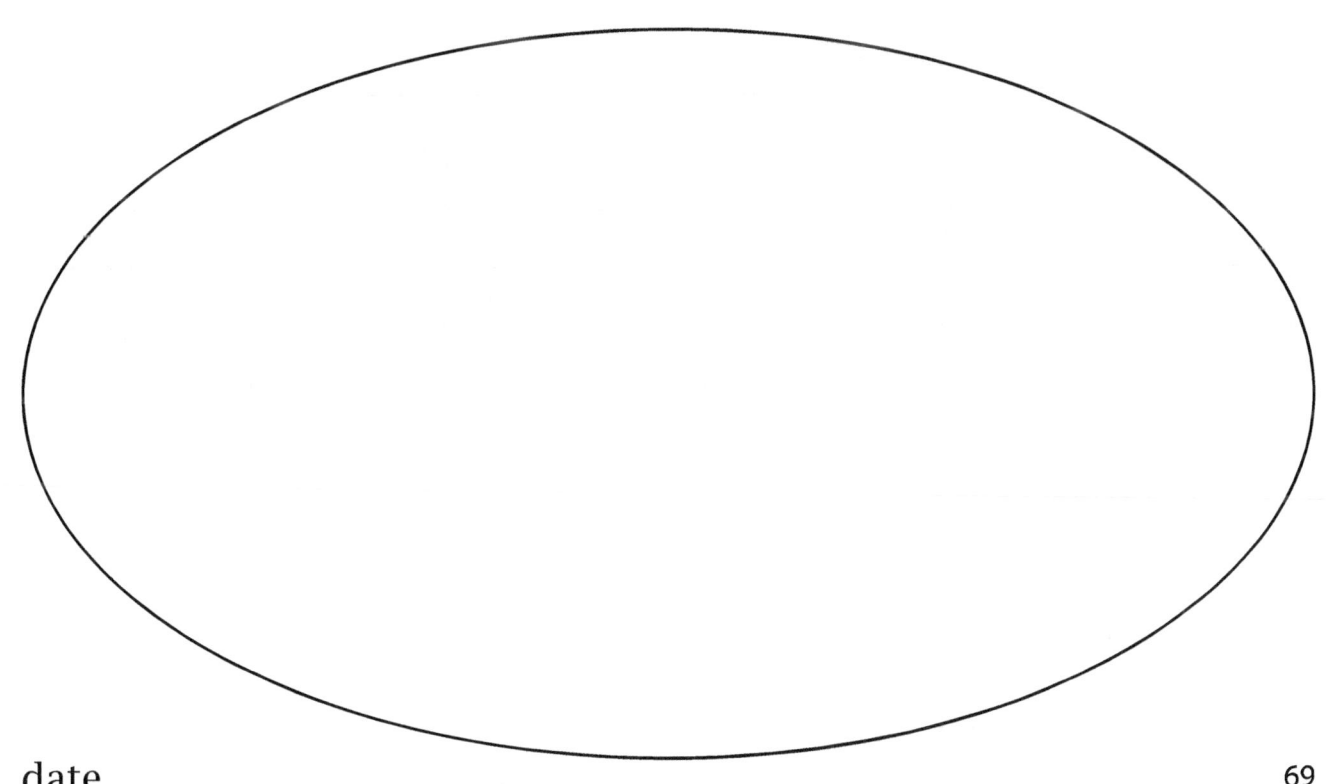

date_____

> *You will find peace not by trying to escape your problems, but by confronting them courageously. You will find peace not in denial, but in victory.*
> *J. Donald Walters*

Write down all those thoughts that are weighing you down. Then let them go.
(optional; cross them out with black ink or do whatever you need to do to let them go)

Make time for peaceful activities.
An action that brought me peace today was...

_____
_____
_____
_____
_____
_____
_____
_____
_____
_____

Art Therapy
Give yourself some time to scribble out those feelings. Either purposefully draw a picture or grab a color, close your eyes and let your mind go.

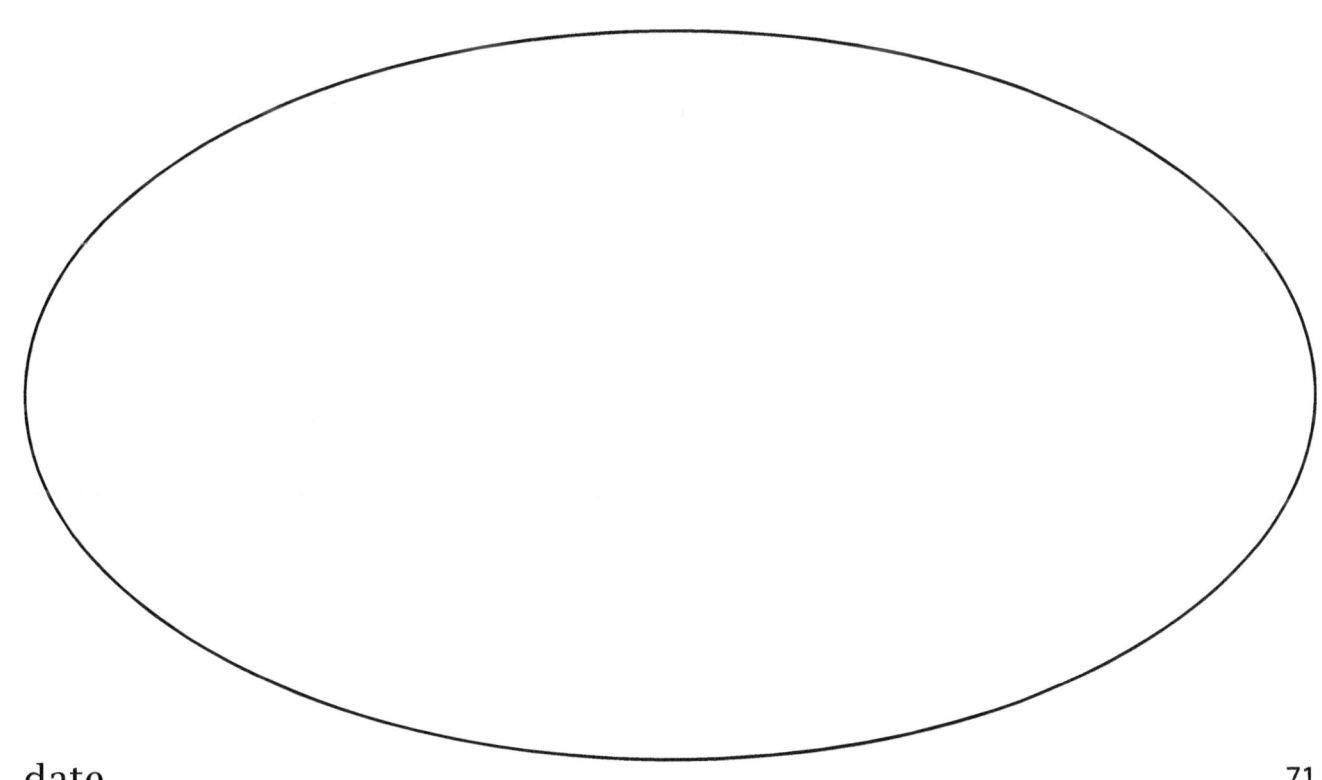

date_____

> *If there is to be any peace it will come through being, not having.*
> *Henry Miller*

Write down all those thoughts that are weighing you down. Then let them go.
(optional; cross them out with black ink or do whatever you need to do to let them go)

Make time for peaceful activities.
An action that brought me peace today was...

_____
_____
_____
_____
_____
_____
_____
_____
_____
_____

Art Therapy
Give yourself some time to scribble out those feelings. Either purposefully draw a picture or grab a color, close your eyes and let your mind go.

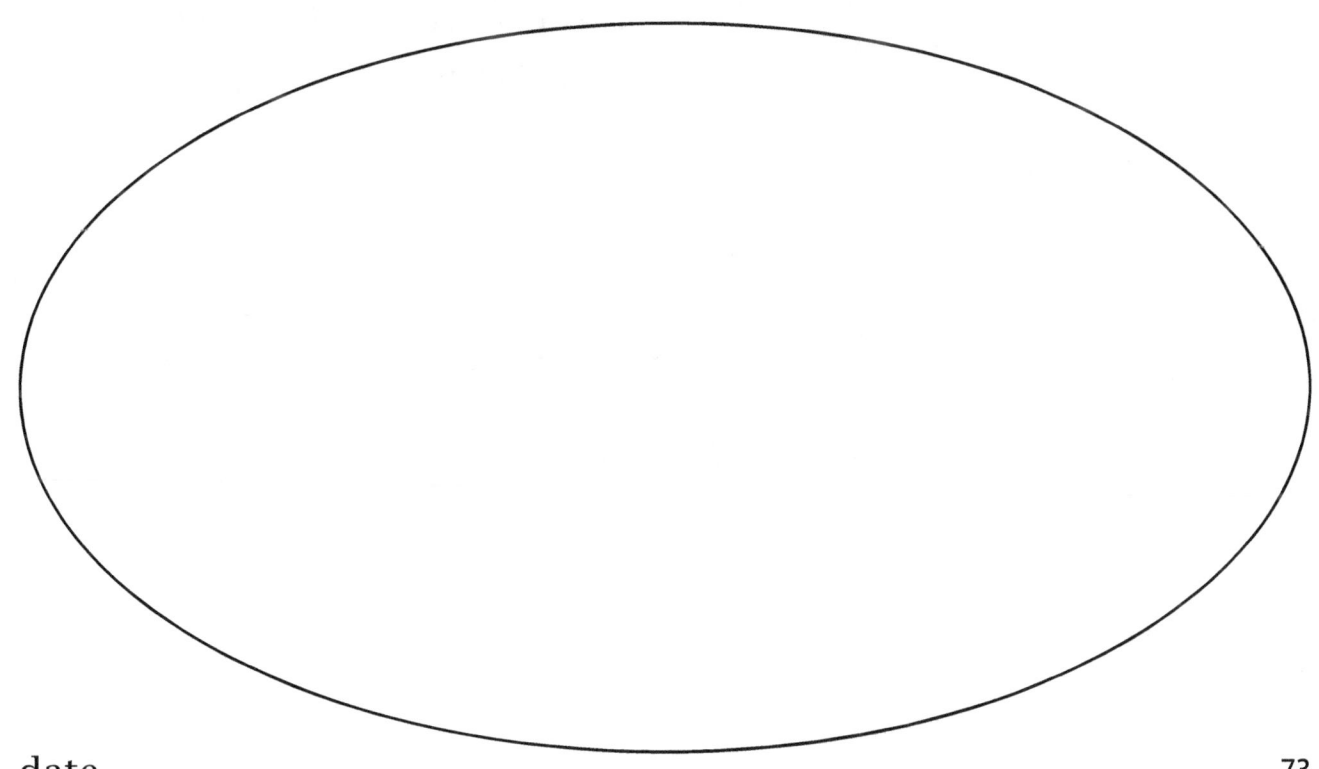

date_____

What a week! I love my peaceful journal.

Write down the difference you notice in your life as you have been focused on peace.

_____
_____
_____
_____
_____
_____
_____
_____
_____
_____
_____
_____
_____
_____

> *Peace is its own reward.*
> *Mahatma Gandhi*

**** *My daily peaceful actions* ****

_____
_____
_____
_____

Dear _____

I have something I need to tell you. I forgive you for...

_____
_____
_____
_____
_____
_____
_____
_____
_____
_____
_____
_____
_____
_____
_____
_____
_____
_____
_____

peaceful meter

| I think I am going to scream | | I am like a cloud floating on a breeze |

> *We are bombarded on all sides by a vast number of messages we don't want or need. More information is generated in a single day than we can absorb in a lifetime. To fully enjoy life, all of us must find our own breathing space and peace of mind.*
> *James E. Faust*

Write down all those thoughts that are weighing you down. Then let them go.
(optional; cross them out with black ink or do whatever you need to do to let them go)

Make time for peaceful activities.
An action that brought me peace today was...

_____
_____
_____
_____
_____
_____
_____
_____
_____

Art Therapy
Give yourself some time to scribble out those feelings. Either purposefully draw a picture or grab a color, close your eyes and let your mind go.

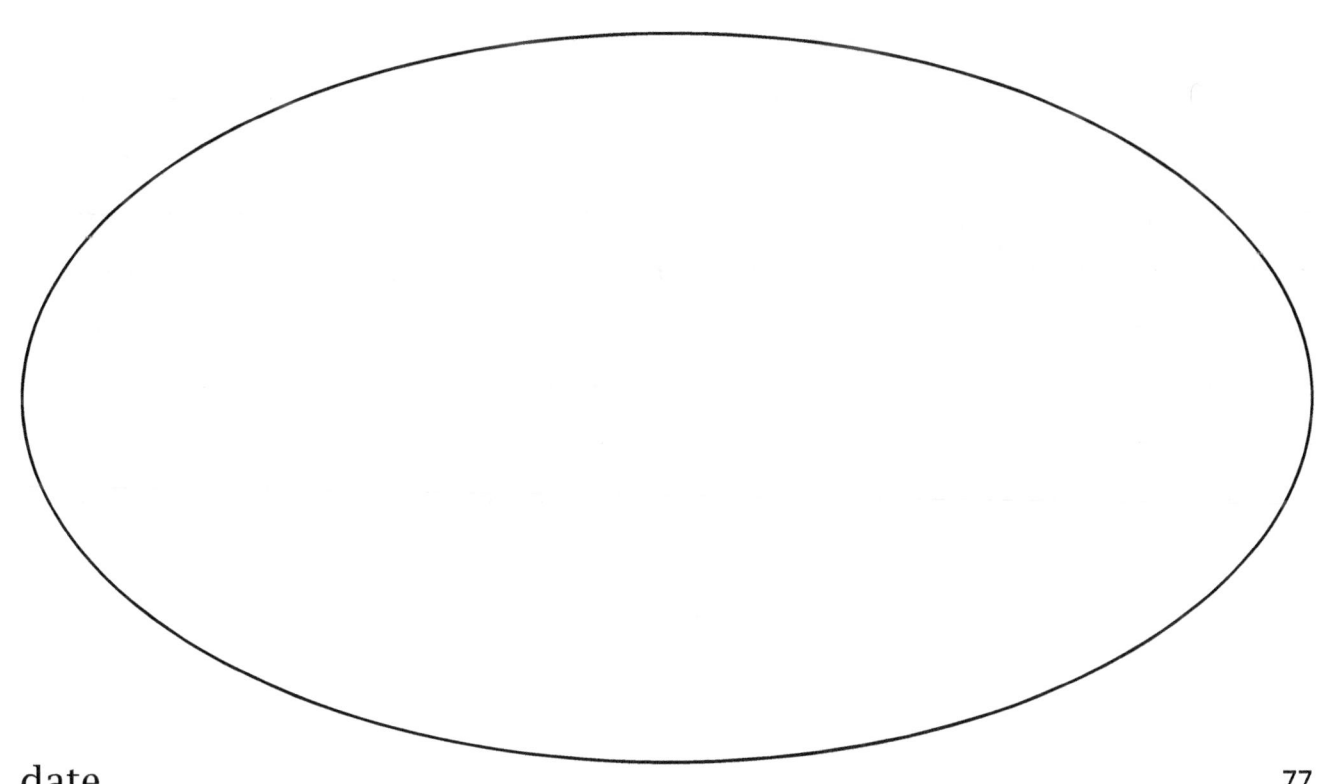

date_____

> *Nowhere can man find a quieter or more untroubled retreat than in his own soul.*
> *Marcus Aurelius*

Write down all those thoughts that are weighing you down. Then let them go.
(optional; cross them out with black ink or do whatever you need to do to let them go)

_____
_____
_____
_____
_____
_____
_____
_____
_____
_____
_____
_____
_____
_____
_____
_____
_____
_____
_____
_____

Make time for peaceful activities.
An action that brought me peace today was...

_____
_____
_____
_____
_____
_____
_____
_____
_____
_____

Art Therapy
Give yourself some time to scribble out those feelings. Either purposefully draw a picture or grab a color, close your eyes and let your mind go.

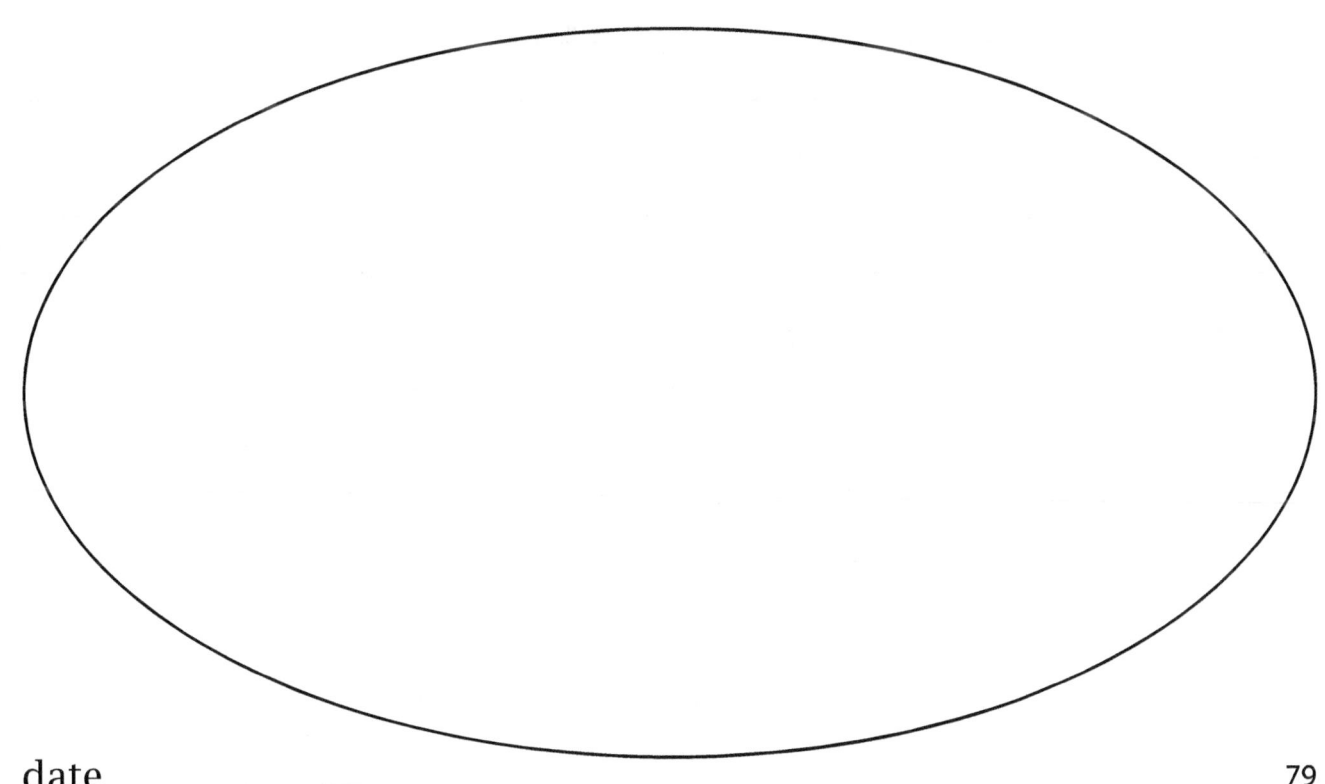

date_____

> *Peace has to be created, in order to be maintained. It will never be achieved by passivity and quietism.*
> Dorothy Thompson

Write down all those thoughts that are weighing you down. Then let them go.
(optional; cross them out with black ink or do whatever you need to do to let them go)

Make time for peaceful activities.
An action that brought me peace today was...

_____
_____
_____
_____
_____
_____
_____
_____
_____
_____
_____

Art Therapy
Give yourself some time to scribble out those feelings. Either purposefully draw a picture or grab a color, close your eyes and let your mind go.

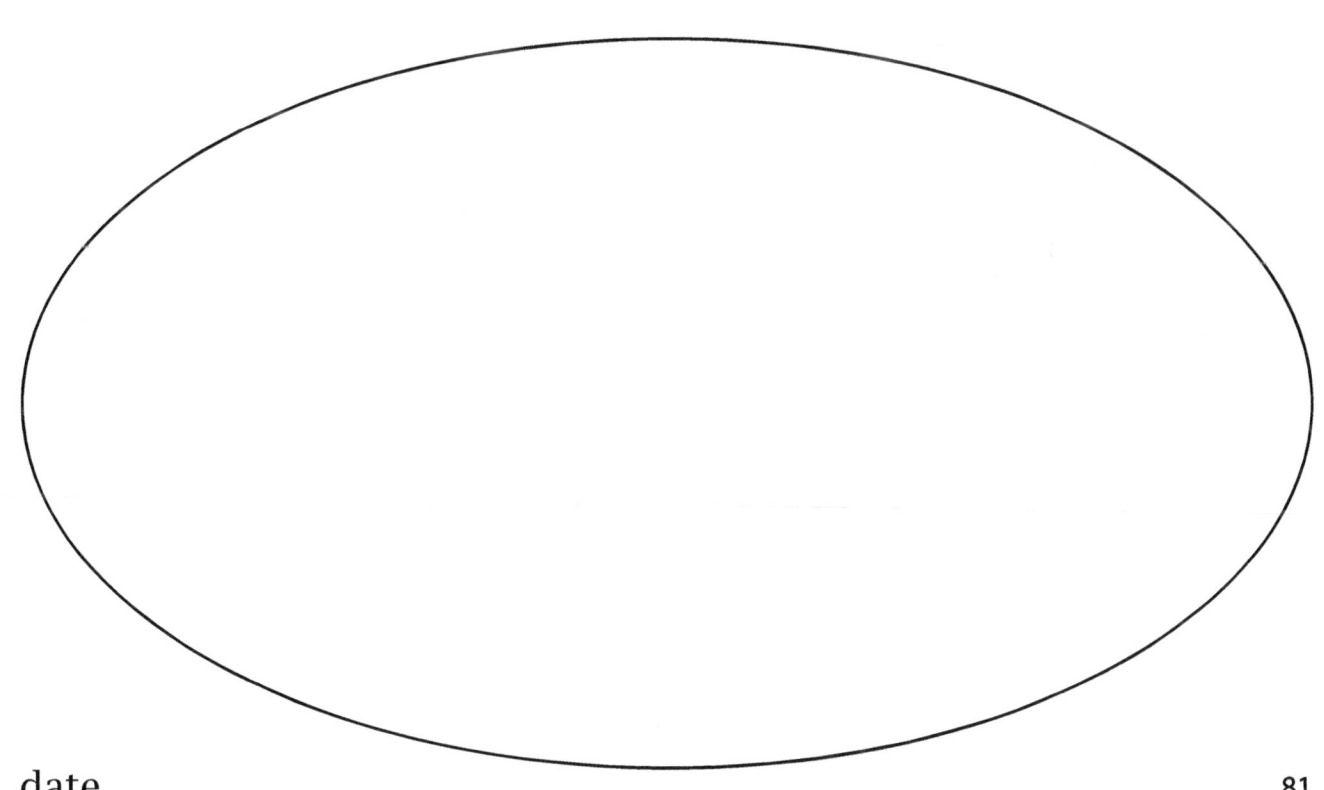

date_____

> *To attain inner peace you must actually give your life, not just your possessions. When you at last give your life - bringing into alignment your beliefs and the way you live then, and only then, can you begin to find inner peace.*
> *Peace Pilgrim*

Write down all those thoughts that are weighing you down. Then let them go.
(optional; cross them out with black ink or do whatever you need to do to let them go)

___
___
___
___
___
___
___
___
___
___
___
___
___
___
___
___
___
___

Make time for peaceful activities.
An action that brought me peace today was...

_____

Art Therapy
Give yourself some time to scribble out those feelings. Either purposefully draw a picture or grab a color, close your eyes and let your mind go.

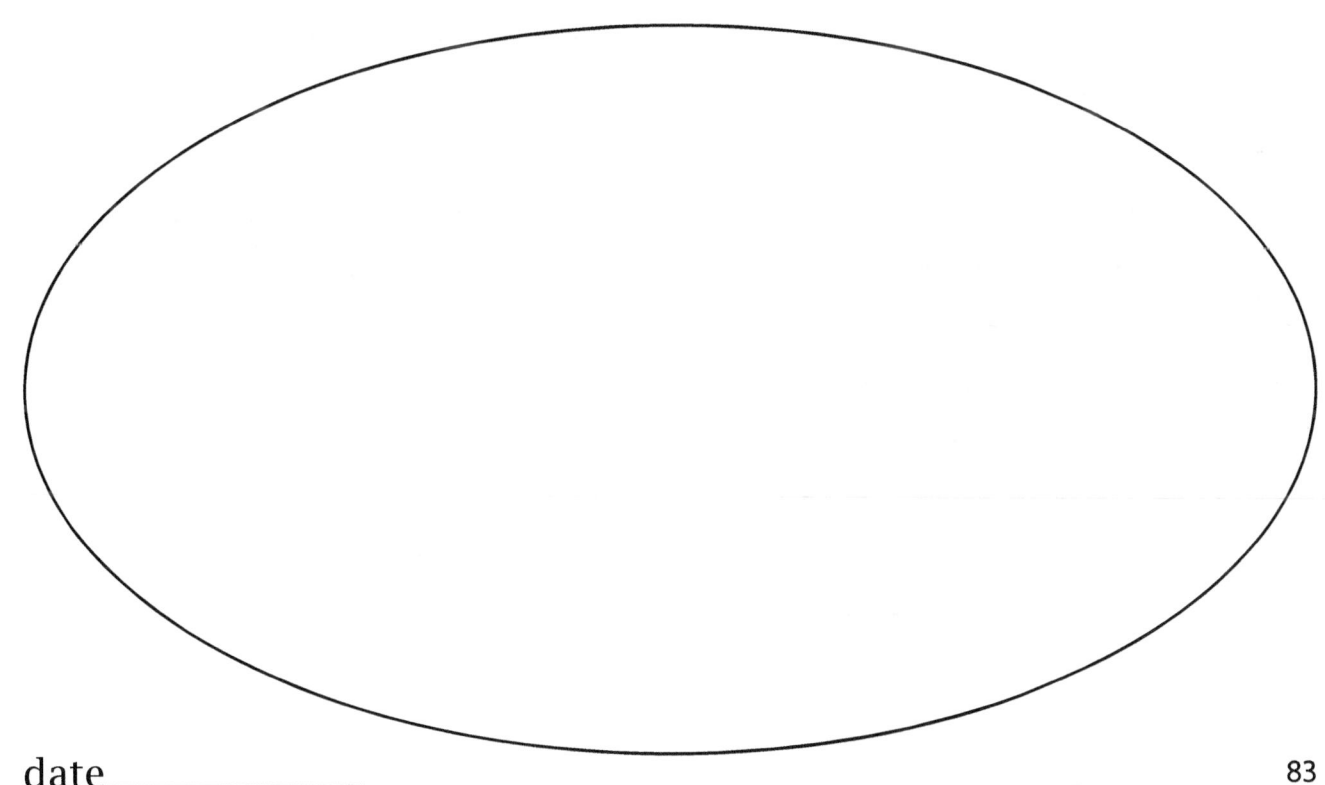

date_____

> *For every minute you remain angry, you give up sixty seconds of peace of mind.*
> *Ralph Waldo Emerson*

Write down all those thoughts that are weighing you down. Then let them go.
(optional; cross them out with black ink or do whatever you need to do to let them go)

_____
_____
_____
_____
_____
_____
_____
_____
_____
_____
_____
_____
_____
_____
_____
_____
_____
_____
_____
_____

Make time for peaceful activities.
An action that brought me peace today was...

_____
_____
_____
_____
_____
_____
_____
_____
_____
_____

Art Therapy
Give yourself some time to scribble out those feelings. Either purposefully draw a picture or grab a color, close your eyes and let your mind go.

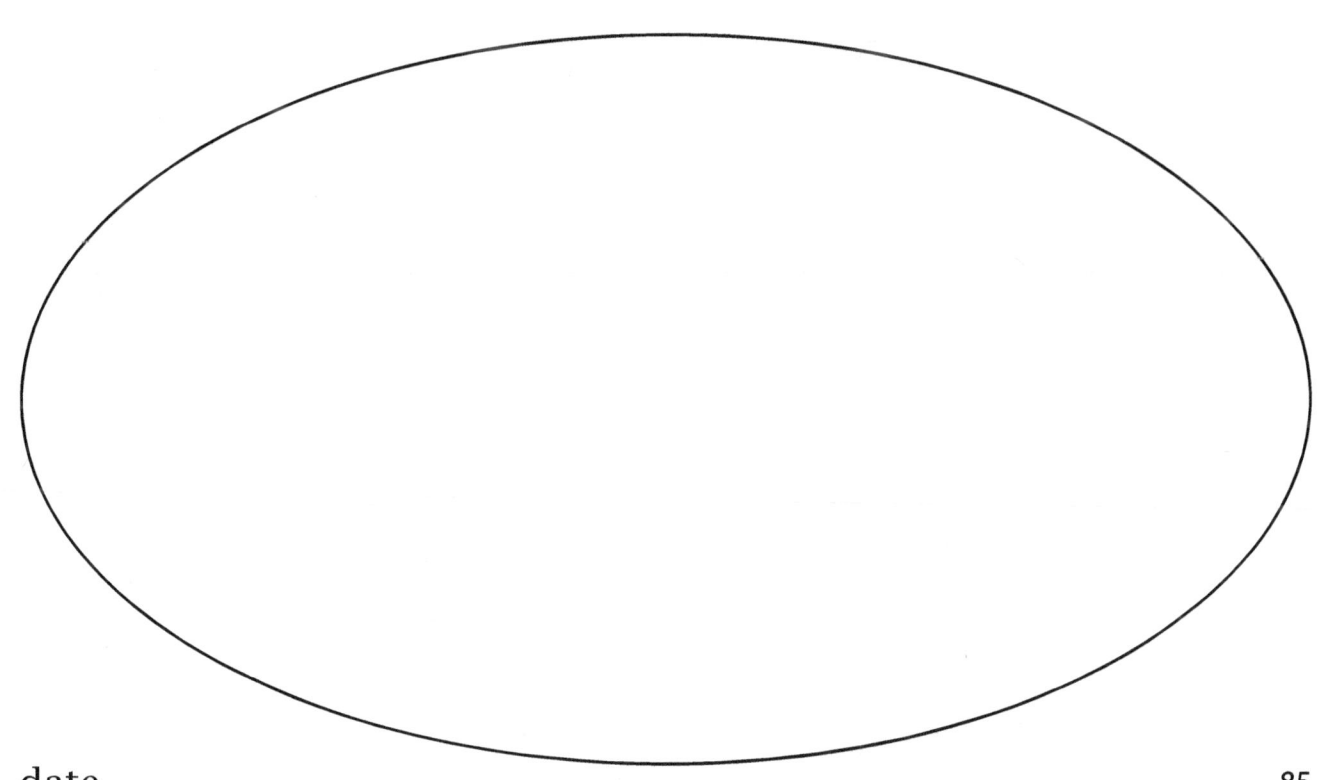

date_____

> *Every goal, every action, every thought,
> every feeling one experiences,
> whether it be consciously or unconsciously
> known, is an attempt to
> increase one's level of peace of mind.*
> *Sydney Madwed*

Write down all those thoughts that are weighing you down. Then let them go.
(optional; cross them out with black ink or do whatever you need to do to let them go)

Make time for peaceful activities.
An action that brought me peace today was...

_____
_____
_____
_____
_____
_____
_____
_____
_____
_____

Art Therapy
Give yourself some time to scribble out those feelings. Either purposefully draw a picture or grab a color, close your eyes and let your mind go.

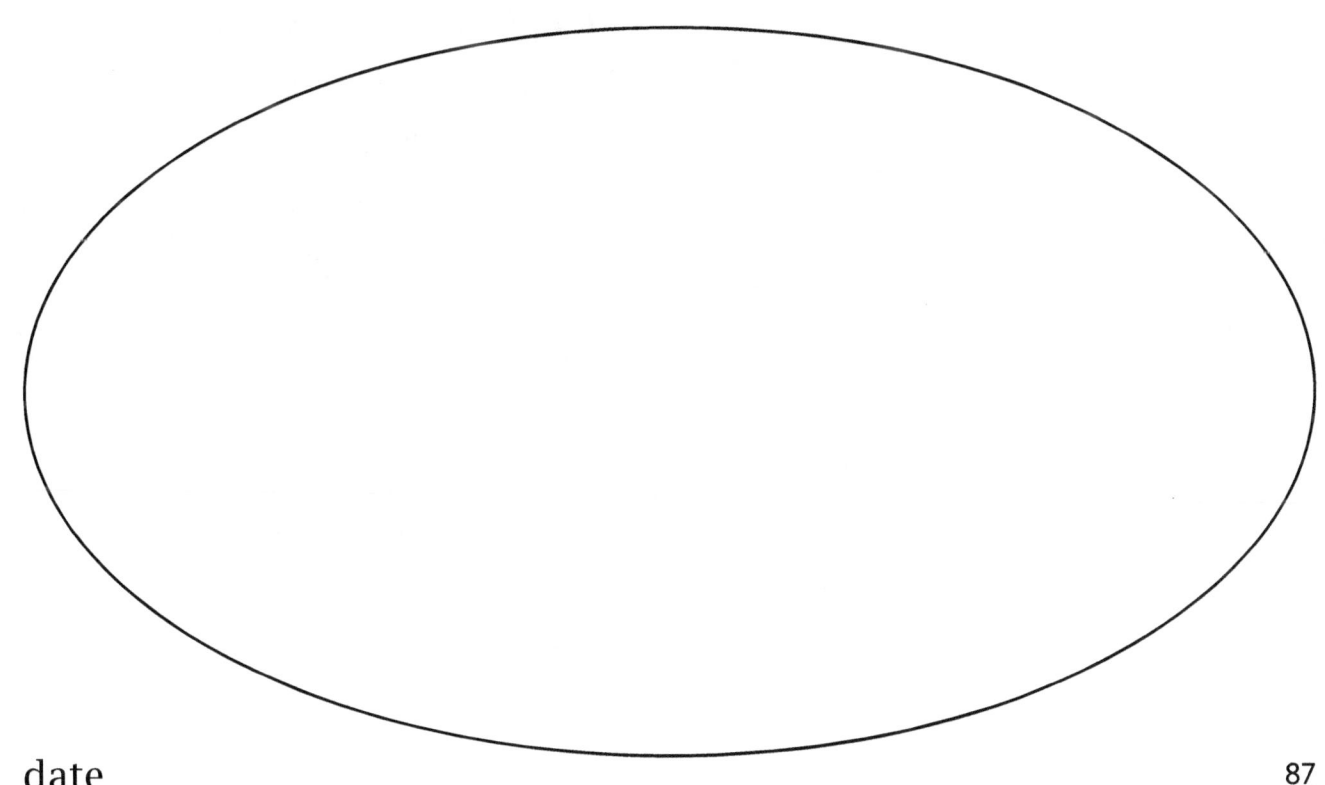

date_____

What a week! I love my peaceful journal.

Write down the difference you notice in your life as you have been focused on peace.

_____
_____
_____
_____
_____
_____
_____
_____

> *Dedicate yourself to the good you deserve and desire for yourself.*
> *Give yourself peace of mind.*
> *You deserve to be happy.*
> *You deserve delight.*
> Hannah Arendt

**** *My daily peaceful actions* ****

_____
_____
_____
_____

Dear _____

I have something I need to tell you. I forgive you for...

_____
_____
_____
_____
_____
_____
_____
_____
_____
_____
_____
_____
_____
_____
_____
_____
_____
_____
_____

peaceful meter

I think I am going to scream │ │ I am like a cloud floating on a breeze

peaceful perceptions, realizations, and notes

peaceful perceptions, realizations, and notes

peaceful perceptions, realizations, and notes

peaceful perceptions, realizations, and notes

peaceful perceptions, realizations, and notes

Available Now
From Uiri Press

The I Am So Happy journal is a 46 day exploration into what makes you happy.

By Sky Hawk

ISBN 978-0-9979051-0-6

The I Am So Grateful journal is a 35 day voyage into bringing more thankfulness into your life.

By Sky Hawk

ISBN 978-0-9979051-1-3

About the Author

Sky Hawk is an author, artist, nature lover, successful entrepreneur, healer, and mother. She is the creator of her life, the I Am So series, herbal tracking journals, and much more. She helps people feel the love in themselves and is a spreader of joy.

www.ingramcontent.com/pod-product-compliance
Lightning Source LLC
Chambersburg PA
CBHW060457300426
44113CB00016B/2625